Running for Office as an Online Candidate

Web Strategies for Local Campaigns

Shane Daley

ISBN: 9781976790294

Daley Professional Web Solutions/Online Candidate
PO Box 402
Montgomery, NY 12549

www.DaleyPWS.com
www.OnlineCandidate.com

NOTICE OF LIABILITY

The author and publisher have made every effort to ensure the accuracy of the information herein. However, the information contained in this book is sold without warranty, either express or implied. Neither the author, nor its dealers or distributors, will be held liable for any damages caused either directly or indirectly by the instructions contained in this book, or by the software or hardware products described herein.

The reader is encouraged to seek competent legal and accounting advice before engaging in any campaign business activity.

Contents

Introduction

When we started Online Candidate in 2003, it was tough to convince local candidates that an online presence could help them win an election. Today, political candidates of all levels realize the power of online campaigning. They use the web to build a volunteer base, raise money, and boost voter support.

From building a campaign website, to social networking, to maintaining an online reputation, there is a lot to do and a lot to know.

With every election cycle the tools, services, and rules change. Keeping up with the digital realm can be a challenge for any political campaign.

> This book is a primer for candidates who want to leverage the web to reach, communicate, and motivate supporters. It is not a comprehensive overview of online marketing. Our goal is to distill the online opportunities, tools, and strategies to help candidates win an election.

Starting early is your best path to success. Read the entire book. Then go through it again and use the checklists to prioritize your efforts. Get others involved, assign responsibilities, and put your plan to work.

Every campaign has a different mix of resources. Not every strategy that is mapped out in this book is necessary to be successful. Apply the ideas that work best for you.

With proper management, you can leverage the web to increase your campaign's online and offline effectiveness. Today, it's not a matter of *whether* you put your campaign online – it's a matter of *how* you do it.

Laying the Groundwork

You, online

In the early 2000s, only the most online-savvy political candidates put much focus on the web. Sure, presidential campaign websites had been around since the mid-90s, but for local candidates the web was not an investment worth spending much time or money on.

How things changed! By 2008, Barack Obama's presidential campaign had raised half a billion dollars online. In 2012, he raised $690 million digitally. By the end of his failed 2016 presidential primary, Bernie Sanders raised $218 million, mostly from small online donations.

Then 2020 changed everything. Health concerns and a deteriorating economy caused by the COVID-19 pandemic reshaped the old political campaign playbook.

Social distancing presented a unique problem for political candidates who spent much of their time interacting with others at campaign events, shaking hands and meeting people face to face.

Candidates were forced to campaign while acknowledging unprecedented social and economic conditions. Campaign staffers were ordered to work from home. Field organizing shifted to texting and phone banking. Almost overnight, digital advertising replaced door-to-door canvassing and in-person events.

It was a seismic shift that would permanently alter online campaigning.

Today, almost all political candidates accept online donations in one form or another. They promote themselves with online advertising and interact through social media. Campaigns organize online and even recruit virtual volunteers who help by keyboard. Even local candidates target individual voters in ways that were unheard of a decade ago.

While a campaign website remains the hub of a candidate's online presence, the work begins on a much more personal level.

The value of social networks

The internet allows candidates to make personal connections with voters - quickly, easily, and inexpensively. Through social networking, you can get to know many people, and even more people will get to know you. You can reach more voters online than you can through a dozen campaign events.

The value in building an online network is that you can begin slowly and go as deep as you want. You can start by putting basic information about yourself on the web. Then you can begin connecting with people you know. As your network develops, these connections help build relationships and start a conversation. *The purpose of engaging others online is to get people to know, like, and trust you.*

Building a strong base of supporters before a campaign is important. Successful candidates start an online presence long before they announce their intention to run for office.

Ultimately, you will ask others to act on your behalf. The individuals with whom you have built a relationship will be called upon to give money, donate time, spread the word and, in the end, *vote for you.*

Social networking made it big in the 2008 presidential race. There were over a million Obama supporters on Facebook. McCain supporters numbered just over 150,000.

Creating your online identity

It doesn't matter if you're new to the web or if you've been online since the days of CompuServe. Odds are there is information about you online that can be accessed with a simple search engine query.

Go ahead and 'google' yourself. Do a search on google.com for your name. What shows up in the results? There might be pages that randomly contain your first and last name. Perhaps you share a name with someone else and results about that other person are showing up.

If that other person is somewhat famous (or infamous), there may be articles, blog posts, or other content about that person. Another reason there might be information online about that person is because they *put* information about themselves on the web. Search engines picked up that information and then provide that content as search results.

As a candidate, you want influence over what people see, hear, and read about you on the web. To do that, you need an *online identity*. Creating an online identity is simple, and you can do it over time. To start, you need a clear purpose. If that purpose is for political reasons, then you want to create a *personal brand*. That means getting yourself – your history and goals – out on the web.

Another purpose of building an online identity is *search result page domination*. This means that when someone searches your name, positive information about you appears in the top search results. This can be information created by others, *or it can be information that you create yourself.*

The first step in creating an online identity is to create *personal profiles* about yourself.

In this case, we are talking about *personal profiles*, not campaign accounts, which have the purpose of promoting you as a candidate. Think of this section as creating your personal online resume.

For our purposes, we want sites that have a high search engine authority and tend to rank well for personal name searches. Many websites fit this criterion, but we are going to start with the following:

- LinkedIn
- About.me
- VisualCV

Here is a brief overview of the sites listed above:

LinkedIn – https://www.linkedin.com/

LinkedIn users tend to be business professionals, but the site can be used by people in any field. With a profile, you can post your resume information and link your profile with others. LinkedIn is discussed in more detail below.

About.me – https://about.me/

This site allows you to create a simple page about yourself. It is a place to showcase who you are and what you do.

VisualCV – https://www.visualcv.com/

This site is designed for job seekers. It features an online resume generator that can include images, video, and links. You can share your profile with a vanity link.

By creating profiles on these types of sites, you can begin to brand yourself online long before you begin campaigning.

There are other profile-building sites, but the ones listed above are free and popular. You may also want to create personal profiles on industry or professional-related sites.

What about Wikipedia?

Almost every Wikipedia page (or Wiki page) tends to rank very well for Google searches. It might seem like creating an entry for yourself on Wikipedia.com is a great idea.

It's not.

Using Wikipedia to put out information about yourself can become a problem. Once a Wikipedia page is created, it is likely to remain there forever. Your page will almost certainly be edited at some point, as anyone can submit changes. Edits can be approved if there is a reliable reference to back up the changes. Potential changes can include positive or *negative* information and citations.

While you may be able to create a Wikipedia page about yourself, *you will never have control over it.*

If a Wiki page already exists about you, you can submit your own updates. Be factual in your edits and avoid anything that smacks of self-promotion. Otherwise, the editors will reject your changes and potentially block your account.

While *online reputation management* is usually associated with businesses, it also applies to individuals. A person can have a great public reputation. Unfortunately, it is impossible to control what others say or post online. One bad post can undo a lifetime of achievement. A negative online reputation can cause embarrassment, cost someone a job, relationships, and future business dealings. Take control of what you can to help maintain a positive online reputation.

The least you need to know

Is it essential to build profiles and put content about yourself online? No, but it will help if you are looking to build a solid online foundation.

In time, profiles will appear in searches related to your name. Where you can, link your profiles together. Cross-linking similar pages builds relevancy for your name. In time, you can also link your personal profiles to your campaign website and social media profiles to also boost their search engine ranking.

> The web is where voters look for political information. If you do not put out information about yourself, *then someone else will.*

Action Steps

- Create personal accounts that will rank well for online searches. Only add information that you are comfortable sharing. Keep in mind that if you are running for public office, there won't be much information about you that *isn't* public.

- Use a consistent name throughout all your profiles. Try to match your future ballot name if you can.

- Include a head shot photo. It should be a recent picture where you are dressed well. A smile always helps, too.

- When you have completed your profiles, go back and cross-link profiles to each other where you can.

- Finally, maintain a list of your profiles and keep them up to date as you move forward.

Creating Your Social Media Presence

In years past, most candidates started social networking after they made the decision to run for office. Social media was an afterthought, a secondary way to drum up support – if they used social media at all.

These days, it is recommended to start an online presence as early as possible. That allows you more time to build a network of friends and supporters.

Building a personal online social presence gives you a leg up when you announce your intention to run for office. Your friends and fans will be the first to check out your campaign website, provide feedback, promote your cause, and help in your fundraising and volunteer efforts.

> Did you know that 72% of U.S. adults have at least one social media account? Source: Pew Research Center, 2019

The dark side of social media

Are you already engaged online? Do you maintain a Facebook or Twitter account? Is there an old MySpace page of yours somewhere? Did you ever post comments on online forums under your own name? If you have ever done any of these things, then you have left behind all kinds of digital footprints that could come back to bite you when you run for office.

Young people tend to put personal information online because they have been exposed to social media earlier in life. At some point they may be older, wiser, and dealing with the consequences of their online activities.

Racy photos, crazy party shots, offensive posts, embarrassing video clips, and discussion board comments can remain online for years. When these digital artifacts are 'discovered', political opponents often use these items out of context (or even *in* context, as the case may be). This can leave candidates confronting sticky issues.

No amount of detergent can provide a digital scrubbing

Deleting online material will not make the information disappear. A saved screen shot, a digital photograph on a hard drive, or even an archived web page on Archive.org may still be out there. Trying to delete material after it is discovered can only inflame the issue and make it seem like a candidate is trying to hide something.

When posting online, use this rule of thumb: Anything that you say or do online will be made public and could be used against you by a political opponent. If you are not comfortable with anyone seeing certain material about you, then do not post it online.

Of course, that doesn't prevent *other people* from posting material about *you*. In this age of viral content, you will want to watch what you do or say in any setting where there is the possibility of you being recorded.

Do not rely on the privacy controls of online services. Privacy policies change, and there is nothing to stop other users from reposting material you've shared.

Fix what you can as early as possible

If you currently use social media sites, consider cleaning up old posts, and watch what you post going forward. Rework slang or colloquial phrasing within your profiles. Update your profile images to ones that better suit a political candidate. Do this as early as possible. You don't have to change who you are but be aware of how you could be presenting yourself to future voters.

No matter what you do, embarrassing online material may be discovered. In the end, it is best to fix what you can, accept what you cannot change, and move on to more important issues. If you believe that existing material will become a problem at some point, figure out ahead of time how you will deal with that.

Again, assume that any online communication you make will become public. Privacy standards shift over time. Information currently walled-off within certain websites might become open at some point.

TECH TIP: During a campaign, you will create several online accounts. For better security, use different passwords on all your accounts. That way, if one account is hacked, the others will not be as vulnerable. Consider using software like *LastPass* to help manage your passwords.

Who should manage your online presence?

You may need help to monitor and post material on behalf of your campaign. Many candidates handle everything themselves, but even a small campaign may have one or more persons who act as an *online coordinator.*

An online coordinator may be tasked with monitoring accounts, creating posts, handling campaign email and newsletters, and perhaps even updating the campaign website. You may decide to have several trusted volunteers help with your online efforts. Everyone should know their duties and what they are authorized to do on behalf of the candidate or campaign. Ongoing communication between coordinators is important.

Online coordinators need access to various accounts. Take care not to allow one person to have too much control. You don't want to be potentially locked out of accounts or unable to post if a coordinator is not available. For better coverage, you may want to have multiple administrators for different accounts.

Give others only as much account control as they require. If someone only needs 'Editor' access to update an account, then don't give them an 'Administrator' role.

Keeping it safe

When setting up accounts, you may want to use a common campaign email account that is controlled only by you or a high-level campaign member. That can help you keep control over everything. At some point, you may need to update login information or remove a coordinator from your accounts.

Most website hosts allow you to create *email forwards* that simply redirect email from one address to one or more other addresses. You can use a different email forward for each social media account. It is easier to update where email forwards point to than to change permissions over actual email accounts.

> Maintain an ongoing list of the information for your various accounts. You should note what individuals have access to any accounts.

Choosing your campaign handles

When you start your online campaign, you will need to pick a website domain name and names (or handles) for your campaign's social media profiles.

The question that often arises is whether you should include the name of the office you are seeking.

For example, should you use the handle *Elect John Smith* or *John Smith for Mayor*?

Avoid using an office name and/or year in your website name and social media handles. It's better to use your name with a more generic 'vote for' or 'elect' prefix.

If you are going to be in politics for a while, odds are that the position you are seeking will change in the future. If that happens, all the work to build your online presence for an old position may go to waste.

For example, you can change the web address on a Facebook Page to a unique username address. However, once you choose a unique address, you might not be able to change it again in the future. A page named *facebook.com/smithforsupervisor* won't work well if you run for a different office. It may be tough to get all your old followers over to a new page.

The same goes for a campaign Twitter account. Your handle *@smithforsupervisor* will look silly when you later run for state representative.

When coming up with your online account names and handles, be sure to choose carefully – and be prepared to keep them for a while.

Don't switch personal social media accounts into campaign accounts. Start fresh and create new social media handles and accounts. Encourage existing friends and contacts from your personal accounts to follow your new campaign accounts.

Creating a Campaign Facebook Account

Facebook.com is the most popular social network today. It is a popular place for campaigns, political parties, and nonprofit groups to build support and promote themselves online. The site allows users to share news, photos, links, and videos with friends and followers.

If you are running for office, maintaining a presence on Facebook is critical. For many people (voters), Facebook has become the *de facto* internet.

> 69% of adults use Facebook. *Source: Pew Research Center, 2021*

Starting with Facebook

Creating a personal Facebook account is simple. Once you have registered and confirmed your email address, you can check for friends on the network.

In your personal profile you can provide information about where you live and went to school. Joining a group for your city is another way to find people you know who are already using the service.

When others accept your 'friend' invitations, you will be able to follow updates they make – and they will be able to do the same with you.

If you plan to use Facebook for your campaign, start early by creating a personal account, and build up your network of friends. That way, you'll learn how Facebook works before you use the platform for political purposes.

Facebook Pages vs personal accounts. With a personal account, you can find friends and post updates to share. Personal accounts are *not* designed for 'public' access. That's what business and organization 'pages' are for. *Pages* are independent and are generally open to any visitor. A personal account is required to create and manage Facebook Pages.

Authorizing your campaign with Facebook

If you use Facebook for your campaign, there is a very good chance that at some point you will want to advertise on the platform.

In an effort at transparency, users who run election-related, referendum or issue ads on Facebook or Instagram must be *authorized*. Any ads that mention a political candidate will have to adhere to these rules. Ads that qualify will have a "paid for by" tag.

To be authorized, you'll need to be an administrator for the Page running the ads. You must also have *two-factor authentication* enabled on your account. Facebook will also need to ensure that you are based in the United States. They will check your information and activity on Facebook and ask for a mailing address. You will also need to provide additional information to confirm your identity.

If you plan on running online ads on Facebook or Instagram, get your organization authorized as soon as possible. The process can take days or even weeks. This process is discussed further below.

For more information, visit the *Facebook for Politics & Government* page at https://www.facebook.com/gpa/.

Campaign Facebook Pages

Facebook Pages are for businesses, organizations, and brands to share their stories and connect with people. They can be used to post content, list events, upload video and more.

Pages are created through personal accounts, though one or more personal accounts can manage a page. Facebook allows you to create a political page only if you are the candidate or an authorized staff member. Facebook will remove fake pages. Users who create fake pages may also have their personal accounts disabled.

Unlike your personal profile, Facebook pages are visible to everyone by default. Any person on Facebook can connect with your page by 'Liking' it. In doing so, they can receive future updates about the page in their news feed, be able to comment and interact on the page, and share updates with their own friends.

There are several things you must do to complete your campaign page:

Upload a cover photo: This can be a campaign logo or a modified version of your campaign website. You can change it as often as you want. Size requirements for cover and profile pictures change often. Check the Facebook help section for the current sizes and restrictions.

Upload a profile picture: Your profile picture appears on Facebook as a thumbnail image in news feed stories, ads, and featured stories. This can be a candidate head shot or logo.

Manage your page settings: Set up page administrators, notifications, preferred audience and more. In the General Settings, review your visitor post settings, profanity filters, and message settings.

Add past events: You can create posts for a candidate's professional and political history and add them to your page timeline.

Post regularly: Posts that include photos or video tend to generate more engagement than other post types.

Highlight a post and "pin" it to the top of your page: A pinned post will stay at the top of your page Timeline. Pinning a call to action to donate or volunteer will keep the request in a prominent position.

Set your template: You can set the page template with default buttons and tabs. The 'Politicians' template is a good choice.

Complete additional information: Fill out the Edit Page Info section as much as you can. Make sure the information you provide matches public records.

For more information on setting up a Facebook Page, visit: https://www.facebook.com/business/pages/set-up

Facebook Events

Facebook events let you organize and respond to gatherings in the real world with people on Facebook.

When creating an event, it should have a clear name, a thorough description and a location. Use an eye-catching photo to make it stand out. When people RSVP for your Facebook event, you can message them with updates, encourage them to share updates, and when you post event updates they will be notified.

Events can be made private or public, though you'll probably want to have your campaign events set as public. That way people can post questions and comments that you can respond to.

Post photos and information about your event before, during, and after the event to build and sustain interest. Share your event updates to your campaign page.

Whenever someone adds a status that they are going to an event or are interested in an event, their friends will see that status in their news feed. This adds a bit of additional publicity.

For more exposure, events can be promoted through paid Facebook advertising. To do this, you'll need to be authorized first.

Facebook Groups

Facebook Groups are a place to communicate about shared interests with others. When you create a group from your profile, you can decide whether to make the group public or private. You may require administrator approval for new members. You can also keep your group private and allow new members by invitation only. Posts by a group appear in the news feeds of its members. Members can also interact and share with others in the group.

Confusion sometimes exits as to the differences between a Facebook Page and a Facebook Group. A *page* is designed to a broadcasting to many or all people. A *group* is meant for collaboration and discussion between people with similar interests. Groups are useful for communicating to a select community of people and encouraging them to take action.

Facebook isn't free

Before you invest the time and effort in building a Facebook presence, understand that you will need to pay if you want your posts and updates to reach others in any significant way.

> Facebook is a pay-for-exposure platform. You will need to promote posts to ensure your messages are seen by your followers and/or other audiences.

Don't assume that people who like your page will see your updates. In fact, most users do not realize that when they

'Like' a page, there is no guarantee that they will see future updates from that Page.

Facebook uses an algorithm to determine the relevancy of every post to a follower. This helps Facebook deliver updates that a person wants to see and filters out the rest.

Facebook does this to prevent news feeds from becoming an endless stream of status updates.

After someone likes your Page, they will probably see your next few posts in their news feed. If they do not interact with your posts, Facebook will assume that person is not interested in your content. In the future they will see fewer posts from you. That's a problem for people who follow your campaign exclusively on Facebook. If they don't regularly see your posts, then they are 'out of the loop'.

The reality is that a typical page post is seen by less than 5% of its followers. This low number is purposeful. Facebook wants Page owners to pay for exposure.

If you use Facebook for your campaign, dedicate a budget to promote your most important posts. That is the only way you can keep a connection with all who follow you.

For authorized users, Facebook offers several advertising options. These are discussed below.

Facebook post ideas

The core of your Facebook presence is in your posts. Posts can include updates from your campaign website, press releases, news articles, event reminders, photographs, personal observations, and more.

Here are some Facebook post ideas:

- Candidate thoughts or comment of the day.

- News articles related to a major campaign issue.

- News about your location/district, with comment.

- (Not so flattering) news about your opponents.
- Requests for followers to stay current by signing up for your email list.
- Reminders about events.
- Follow-ups about events.
- Latest poll numbers about you.
- Latest poll numbers about your opponent.
- Polls about issues important to your followers.
- Links to your latest website content.
- Blog posts on other sites about you or your campaign.
- Volunteer requests - usually tied to a specific event or activity.
- Updates about campaign staff that may be of general interest.
- Fundraising goal status.
- Notification of new billboard/large banner location.
- Announcement that signs are available.
- Links to new video or campaign ads.
- Links to brochure or position paper files on your campaign website or elsewhere.
- Latest endorsement announcements.
- Thank you to helpful supporters/organizations.

Viral and 'sharable' content is valuable. It strengthens affinity and increases the chance of future posts showing up in the news feeds of your followers.

Three types of posts tend to attract more engagement:

Images: Strong visuals tends to go viral. Focus on catering to voter interests with relevant and appealing images or graphics. Don't forget to include strong calls to action such as "Donate Now" or "Share this with a friend". Consider watermarking images for branding in case they are shared.

Open-ended questions: Yes/No questions are easy to answer, but provocative questions tend to get better responses and more shares. This applies to both posts and online polls.

Video: Consider using video teasers – 1 to 3 minutes in length – rather than long videos. Share an interesting message or story that relates to your constituents. Videos directly uploaded to Facebook tend to perform better than videos linked from other sources. You can record and upload or record through Facebook Live, discussed below.

You will only learn what works by experimenting. If something does well, resist the urge to overdo it. They say variety is the spice of life – and the same goes for online marketing.

Try different ideas and topics to determine what makes people react. The frequency of your updates should depend on your audience. The more followers who interact with your posts, the more people will be exposed to your messages.

Using multiple Facebook Pages

Perhaps one Facebook page for your campaign is not enough. To create a larger 'brand' footprint and have more niche interaction, consider launching multiple pages that address a specific issue or topic.

Separate pages are good for:

- **Negative material that you don't want to post on your primary page.** "What is Candidate X hiding?" or "How Much Has Candidate X Spent This Week?" make for interesting topics.

- **Pages that relate to a constituency or group**. If you want to target a specific issue, you could break it out to a separate page. You can also create special pages for targeted audiences or constituencies. For example, "The War of Candidate X on..." or "Candidate X Supports...".

It is better for each page to have an ongoing, specific theme. Be sure to keep them updated. Resist the urge to create multiple pages without a clear purpose and content plan.

Sometimes pages or specific posts may go viral and attract feedback. Be prepared to monitor your social media accounts and respond as necessary.

Using a timeline to slam your opponents

Facebook's Timeline format opens opportunities for political campaigns. Using the Timeline, you can add events, links, and messages to your wall or a page. You can post items that go back years – as far back as the year 1000 AD. Posts are displayed in chronological order down the page.

A timeline is a great way to select and organize events in a way that can help your campaign – or slam your opponents.

One of the first instances of a political Facebook Timeline was in 2012. Newt Gingrich used a page to chronicle Mitt Romney's past gaffes and alleged flip-flops. Old news articles and videos with commentary created a selective history for primary voters.

This technique is an alternative to building a microsite (described below). For example, a page timeline can encapsulate:

- An opponent's campaign gaffes or flip-flops

- A timeline of an opponent's reaction to an issue or event

- To set the record straight about the candidate or an opponent

- History of a term in office

- Donor or support history

If you have done your opposition research, then you may already have plenty of good material. If you have several topics to cover, you may want to create separate pages. Each post and comment should reinforce the point you are trying to make.

Facebook optimization tips

Optimizing your page content will help your page rank for relevant searches on Facebook and search engines.

Choose the right page title. This is the most basic step when optimizing for Facebook. Keep your page name simple. "Elect John Smith" works well.

Include keywords. Besides using your name in the page title, include your name and elected position in your page description. To optimize your page for local searches, include address information in the additional information sections.

Create a custom vanity URL. Once your page has been around for a short time, Facebook lets you create a unique URL (or username) for the page. Again, keep it simple. Something like 'facebook.com/electjohnsmith' is both descriptive and generic enough to be useful now and in the future.

Add a cover image. A cover image is the largest visual element that sits at the top of your page. Most candidates use a variation of their signage. Others get more creative.

Your cover photo will look best if it is optimized with the right dimensions. These dimensions have changed several times over the years. For details on the current sizes, type 'cover size' into the Facebook help search box.

Cover photos are public, which means anyone visiting your page can see it. They cannot be deceptive, misleading, or infringe on any copyright.

Get your timeline in order. Highlight events or actions that help give a narrative or tell a story about you or your campaign.

Build backlinks to your Facebook page. Good links will help your page rank better and help tie your page to other aspects of your online presence. Link to your page from your campaign website and other profiles you control. Done properly, your page should rank well for candidate name searches. (And don't forget to add your campaign website link to your page's 'Info' section.)

Additional Facebook tips

- Don't post remarks or upload photos that you might later regret. Nothing really disappears on the web, and that off-color 'joke' you made months ago could come back to haunt you.

- Voters value authenticity from politicians who use social media.

- If you are not sure what to post or promote, follow the examples of other popular candidates.

Facebook is constantly evolving. For the latest Facebook information and tips, visit https://www.facebook.com/help/.

Facebook metrics

A lot of planning goes into Facebook marketing. To make it work right, you need to measure results.

So, what is the most important thing you should track in your Facebook Page Insights?

Hint: It's not your number of followers.

Each page provides usage information that you can view online or download as a multi-tab spreadsheet. You can find this in the *Insights* section.

Pay attention to the "Posts" section. This information will help you understand what types of posts are resonating with your fans, how they are interacting with your posts, and how you are getting your messages to go viral. This will also tell you if your advertising is driving new fans, shares, and interactions.

Make use of landing pages when you drive traffic from Facebook. This means creating specific web pages for different requests. That way you can determine the effectiveness of your Facebook marketing. The concept of landing pages is explained in further detail below.

You can track *conversions* (email signups, donations, etc.) from Facebook traffic by adding a small amount of code to a separate 'conversion page'. This could be your email sign-up thank you page or your donation confirmation page.

Find out more about the tracking pixel at:

https://www.facebook.com/business/help/742478679120153

For more information on Facebook Insights, visit:

https://www.facebook.com/help/268680253165747

Using Facebook Live

Facebook Live allows you to live-stream video directly from a camera, computer, or mobile device to an audience through Facebook. Live broadcasts can be made through your personal Facebook profile, a page, group or even an event. Viewers can watch from their computer, mobile phone or other connected devices.

If you have ever done a video chat with friends or family through Facebook, then you have already used Facebook Live. However, campaign broadcasting is not usually as casual as personal communication. You can use Facebook Live to record and stream a variety of campaign-related material. It is not particularly difficult, and you don't need a full studio setup. In many cases, you can use a mobile device to broadcast.

You can either stream at a particular time or preschedule a time for a live stream. There are plenty of topics for creating live videos:

- Campaign events, rallies, and fundraisers
- Canvassing activities
- Online town hall
- Participation at public meetings or legislative sessions
- Behind the scenes of the campaign
- Personal candidate updates
- Reminders/Get out the vote

Facebook Live videos often seem spontaneous, but for best results you will want to plan each broadcast. For example, randomly filming a canvassing walk might not be interesting. But if you have a topic to discuss or something interesting to show during your walk, that will give your broadcast a purpose. You might not need a full script, but you should have an idea of what's going to happen before you turn on the camera.

A live event can be created from a page or group. You can either go live immediately or schedule your video for a later time. The more information you include when you set up your event, the better. Add a descriptive title and image, mention any special guests, and provide a call to action. This call to action might be to have viewers follow you on social media, volunteer to help or to donate. If you have a poll or questions to add, you can add them when you set up your event.

Announcing your broadcasts ahead of time helps build anticipation and buzz. Post upcoming announcements to your social media accounts. Notify your email subscribers and website visitors. Build anticipation for your events to encourage more viewers.

Once your live stream broadcast is finished, your video is automatically posted to your timeline and saved to your Facebook video library. From there, it can be viewed by others in the future.

You can also download your video to tighten it up and perhaps add an intro and outro (beginning and end branding clips). Then you can upload the edited video to your campaign's YouTube account and embed it into your campaign website. For more control over your embedded videos, consider using a paid video hosting platform like *Wistia* or *Vimeo*.

Regularly check your stats and feedback to see what your content audience engages with the most. You don't want to become repetitious, but you will probably find that certain topics or video types tend to do better than others.

> Remember, you are running for elected office, not for social media influencer. Likes, shares and retweets don't count as votes on Election Day.

Video broadcasting tips

- Make a few practice recordings to get used to speaking in front of a camera.

- Place and settings are important. Choose a proper location that is not too busy or too loud.

- Compose your shots. For example, placing your subject one third to the left or right is more visually interesting than having the subject in the center of the frame.

- Proper lighting is required, especially if you are recording indoors. You may want to add artificial lighting from one or more sources.

- Use quality microphones. Poor audio can provide a worse experience for viewers than even low-resolution video.

- Run a quick trial video before your event and play it back to make sure everything is working properly. There is nothing worse than starting a video and finding out a few minutes later that your audience cannot hear or see you.

- Make sure your internet connection is solid. You don't want to get dropped in the middle of your recording. Depending on your broadcast settings, an unexpected drop-off could terminate your entire event.

Creating a Campaign Twitter Account

Twitter.com is a popular service that allows users to blog in a micro format. Users can 'follow' others and others can follow them back. They post status updates, or 'tweets', which are limited to 280 characters. These updates are communicated to followers, who can read, respond, and share the tweets with others.

Twitter is used by individuals, businesses, and of course, politicians. Twitter presents great opportunities for candidates to enhance branding and build exposure.

Many news organizations follow political Twitter accounts. For candidates and organizations, it's a fast, easy way to broadcast their latest news and messages.

> About 22% of U.S. adults use Twitter. *Source: Pew Research Center, 2019*

Here is a breakdown on how to use Twitter:

Claim @YourCampaign. Even if you don't plan to use Twitter right away, be sure to claim your name or campaign name as your Twitter handle. If you put it off, there's a risk that your name could be taken by someone else. Some candidates use their existing personal account when they run for office, but we advise creating a new account for your campaign. An advantage to using a variant of your name (@JoeSmith or @VoteJoeSmith) rather than a year (@JoeSmith2020) or a position (@Smith4Mayor) is that the account name and link won't become outdated in the future.

Modify your account settings and look. Complete your Twitter profile. Add a photo and a short bio. Include the URL for your campaign website. Brand your Twitter page by customizing the colors and header image. This will help create a look consistent with your campaign design.

Update regularly. Maintaining a Twitter account does not take much time. How often you tweet is less important than posting regularly, no matter what the schedule may be. Due to the continual streaming of Twitter, you can tweet a dozen times a day and not bother most followers.

Post relevant material. Candidates don't have to just post updates on what they are doing or thinking. Look at how other prominent politicians use Twitter for style and content ideas. News articles, campaign press releases, endorsements, website updates, blog posts, and event alerts are all good material to keep followers up to date.

Know the language. Use *hashtags*, *retweets*, and shortened links to give variety to your posts. Don't know what those things are? It's not as complicated as you may think. Check out the Twitter glossary at https://help.twitter.com/en/glossary.

Build your following. Personal contacts will likely be your initial followers. Once you are up and running, Twitter will provide recommendations of others to follow. If you do this, some of these people will follow you back. This will help expose you to others interested in following your campaign. Another tip is to like posts from others. That tends to get attention and sometimes a follow.

Post efficiently. Because you are limited in the number of characters you can make on a Twitter post, you will need to shorten most links you share. Tools to shorten and track your URLs include bitly.com and tiny.cc. Hootsuite.com allows you to shorten URLs and broadcast messages across multiple social media accounts.

> *Always consider what you are saying before you post.* Tweets can be difficult to permanently remove. You can delete a tweet from your account, but others can easily retweet or screen-capture your original post.

Using #hashtags in your campaign

Hashtags are a great way to create a Twitter conversation or be included as a part of a larger conversation. Your tweets have a higher chance of being retweeted when you use the right hashtag to share comments or insights about a topic.

Creating a hashtag is simple. Add a "#" symbol in front of a word or a group of words with the spaces between them taken out.

By including a relevant hashtag, your tweet becomes visible to anyone searching for that topic. It will add your voice to the discussion.

Political campaigns may use a variety of hashtags. Some are general, some specific. For example, there's #election2020, #voting, and so on. You can even create your own hashtag. You might want to make it issue or location-specific, such as #tinytowntraffic, #smithspending or #nonewtaxes.

To get started, check to see if the hashtag(s) you have in mind are already in use. Twitter.com/explore and Hashtags.org are tools you can use for a quick hashtag check.

When you start tweeting with your hashtag, set the context of your hashtag by explaining what it means in the first few tweets.

To keep up with the conversation, you can set up automatic alerts that email you when others tweet or retweet your hashtag. This can be done through posting tools or through services like warble.co.

Twitter tweet ideas

Twitter is designed for 'small bites' of information. You can update your status more frequently than you would on Facebook without annoying your followers.

Here are some things you can promote on Twitter:

- Candidate thoughts or comment of the day.
- News articles related to a major campaign issue.
- News about your location/district, with comment.
- (Not so flattering) news about your opponents.
- Requests for followers to stay current with your campaign by signing up for your email list.
- Reminders about events.
- Live tweets during events.
- Follow-up tweets about events.
- Latest poll numbers about you.
- Latest poll numbers about your opponent.
- Your latest site updates.
- Blog posts on other sites about you or your campaign.
- Volunteer requests tied to a specific event or activity.
- Updates about campaign staff that may be of general interest.
- Fundraising goal status.
- Notification of new billboard/large banner locations.
- Announcement that signs are available.
- Links to new video or campaign ads.

- Links to brochure or position paper files on your campaign website or elsewhere.

- Latest endorsement announcements.

- Thank-you notes to helpful supporters/organizations. (Don't forget to use the @recipient in the message.)

How often should you tweet? That's up to you but you can easily tweet 7-10 times a day. Not everyone will see all your tweets, so you can share some content multiple times throughout the day. If you do this, change up the wording a bit each time.

Common Twitter mistakes

While Twitter is simple to use, you'll want to avoid these common mistakes:

Tweeting from the wrong account: Many people have multiple Twitter accounts. They may have a personal account, a campaign account, and even a business account. *Make sure you are logged into the proper account before you tweet.* This mistake happens more often than you may think.

Confusing a direct message and a general tweet: Many politicians have learned the hard way the difference between a direct message to an individual and a general tweet to your followers. Make sure that you know who you are sending your messages to. Even then, never assume that electronic communications will be kept private.

Being overly emotional: A little emotion in your tweets is fine. You don't want to give the impression that you are a campaigning robot. But too much complaining, vitriol, and anger can come across badly. Keep your language clean, no matter what.

Letting the numbers fool you: The quality, not quantity, of your followers is important. You're running to win an election, not an online popularity contest. Few voters count social media followers as a way of determining who they will support.

Tweeting too little: Don't leave your followers hanging. They might think you've dropped out of the race.

Unimportant tweets: Worse than tweeting too little is tweeting about things that are unimportant or mundane. Nobody cares about what you are eating or drinking for lunch or general comments about the weather.

Spamming: Spamming is blatant and repeated promotional messages. Requests for support are fine. *Lots* of them are fine. However, promotional tweets should be balanced with actual news and insight. What's the ratio? Hard to say, but a 50/50 split could work for campaigns. Also, don't tweet the exact same messages over and over. Even if you are asking for the same thing (such as donations or volunteers), vary your pitch a bit.

Using the @message incorrectly: If you are trying to promote someone like @myfriend, do *not* start your tweet with someone's Twitter handle (@something). If you do that, the only people that will see this message are you, the person you are promoting, and others that follow *both* accounts. Instead of putting the twitter handle at the beginning of the tweet, put it further back in the message.

*Incorrect: @mybuddy has great campaign coverage –
check it out https://bit.ly/LiNk*

*Correct: Read @mybuddy for great campaign coverage.
https://bit.ly/LiNk*

Not leaving enough room for others to retweet: Packing your messages into the maximum length makes it harder for others to retweet. It forces them to shorten your message to resend it to their followers.

> **Be careful what you retweet.** It's tempting to quickly retweet funny memes or negative content about an opponent. Always check the source and author of any material you retweet. You can damage your campaign's credibility by retweeting false or fake content.

Twitter optimization tips

Here are some Twitter optimization tactics to build more traffic and exposure:

Optimize your profile: Add your website link on your profile page and add a bio with the year, elected position sought and location. You'll also want to change the default background and use an appropriate profile image.

Share useful content: Re-tweeting other's posts will help build your brand. Retweet outside posts, such as negative articles about your opponent.

Add more than just text and links: Adding images and video to your tweets makes them likely to be read and shared.

Use Hashtags: Hashtags work like metadata for your tweets. They help organize tweets and determine trending information on Twitter. Locations, issues, and existing hashtags will help you get attention from interested parties.

Follow others: Follow other people and organizations who may be interested in your campaign. Some will follow you back.

Respond to others: Social media is a two-way street. Take the time to respond to any mentions. This is a large part of Twitter and important to growing your connections.

Mention others and ask them to mention you: Don't be afraid to mention others in your tweets. Ask others to retweet your posts, as well. The more your posts are mentioned, the more exposure you will get from others.

Tweet regularly: Don't bulk-post tweets in a short period of time. Instead, spread your tweets out throughout the day. Tools like Hootsuite allow you to set up and schedule tweets ahead of time.

Promote your account: Include your Twitter link on your website, in your email signature, and on your print materials.

Spy on opponents with Twitter

Because much of the data from Twitter is freely available, you can use that information to get an inside look at what your political opponents are saying, planning, and doing.

Before you start, make sure that you already have a Twitter account. It doesn't have to be (and probably shouldn't be) your campaign Twitter account. Create a *private list* in the account and name the list something generic. Add your opponent(s) Twitter feeds to that list. You can also search hashtags and add them to your lists as well.

Now you have an ongoing stream of information that you can use to keep up on specific individuals and topics.

> The default setting for any List is public (anyone can follow the List). To make the List only accessible to you, change the setting to Private.

Private lists can also be created through management clients, such as HootSuite.com or Tweetdeck.com.

Creating a Campaign Google Account

As the largest search engine on the web, we strongly advise creating a new Google account (and Gmail address) for your campaign.

Gmail is a free email service with a large storage capacity. A campaign email address will help separate your personal and campaign activities. It is also easier to allow other campaign staff access to a dedicated account.

> **TIP:** You can use a campaign Gmail account for your campaign's online accounts. Make sure this Gmail address is only accessible by trusted staff. You can use also email forwards from your campaign website domain (socialmedia@mywebsite.com) to redirect incoming email to your Gmail account.

You can sign up for a Google account here:

https://accounts.google.com/signup/

A Google account provides you with access to many other services, including:

- **Google Analytics:** Understanding visitor behavior is the key to a strong campaign website. Google Analytics shows you how visitors are interacting with your site in a variety of ways. With Analytics, you can learn more about your online donations, volunteers, and what drives your site's traffic.

- **Google Search Console** tools and reports help you measure your site's search traffic and performance, fix issues, and improve your site's Google search results.

- **Google Ads:** As your campaign progresses, you can use Google Ads to promote your campaign and specifically target voters by location and by search terms. For example, when someone searches for you on Google, your campaign ad can appear. Online advertising helps build awareness and can even help with your GOTV efforts. This is discussed in more detail below.

- **Google Calendar:** Use this organizing tool to share your schedule with your campaign staff and contacts. You can integrate your calendar with Gmail and view your schedule from within your mailbox.

- **YouTube:** Upload campaign videos to the world's largest video portal using your Google account. Uploaded videos can be embedded into the pages of your campaign website.

- **Google Docs:** Create your own documents, spreadsheets, presentations, and forms that accept user input. You can share these documents with others.

Additional tools can also be of use to your campaign, such as Webmaster Tools, chat and more.

Find tips and tools for protecting your campaign data:

https://protectyourelection.withgoogle.com/intl/en/

Creating a Campaign YouTube Account

Owned by Google, YouTube.com is the web's most popular video-sharing website. Users can view, upload, and share videos. Creating a YouTube account is free and simple. If you have a Google or Gmail account, then you already have account access to YouTube.

When you upload videos, you can share them through social media and even embed your videos into your campaign website. Small campaigns may not generate a huge amount of video traffic. However, the medium can be effective even with a limited audience.

Paid features allow campaigns to promote videos, add call-to-action overlays and run video in-stream ads on YouTube and partner sites.

YouTube optimization tips

Here are techniques to push your video content to the top of the search results on YouTube and Google.com.

Use keywords in your video file name: If you are uploading a video about the 'TinyTown Traffic', then the file name of the video should be something like *tinytown-traffic-problems.mpg*. The file name is not seen by viewers, but YouTube uses words in the file name as part of its ranking algorithm.

Optimize your video titles: Only the first 50 characters or so show up in universal search results. Make the start of the title interesting to attract clicks.

Use detailed descriptive text: Add a link in your video description. This can be your campaign website or another web page. Use 'https://' in the link so it becomes clickable. Then include a keyword-rich description describing your video and your campaign or organization. If you have a script for the video, consider adding it to the video description.

Use the right tags: Video tags help YouTube suggest "Related Videos" that appear when someone watches a video. Tags can include the candidate's name, the campaign, issue-related terms, location, opponent's name, etc. You can be expansive in using them.

Use closed captions: The button 'CC' in the bottom bar of YouTube videos stands for closed captions. YouTube has speech recognition technology that can automatically detect the start and end of each line spoken and match captions to the video's audio. All you need to do is upload a script of the video and the captions will appear in sync with the video.

Embed and Share Your Videos: Keep your channel clean. Avoid posting irrelevant or unrelated videos to your channel. Doing this may dilute the optimization of your other videos. It's better to start a new channel of related videos than to create a single mashup channel.

Drive conversions: Every video you create should push YouTube viewers to do something. Motivate viewers to do something that will help your campaign. Calls to action include donating, volunteering, visiting another website, or to just share the video with others.

You can link to a specific time in the video by adding the code #T=XMYY to the end of the link, where X stands for the number of minutes and YY stands for the number of seconds. For example, #T=3M15 means three minutes and fifteen seconds.

To better influence the related videos that appear, use a similar file name for each of your videos. Use a code that no other YouTube video is going to have, and then append that code to the end of the file name.

Use YouTube Insights to find out more about your audience. The hotspots feature tells you where viewership drops off when viewing a video. This can give you a better idea of optimal video length.

YouTube provides some easy and free editing options. You can trim, remove sections, layer text, and even blur parts of your video. It would be great if you could make layered text a clickable link, but that is not an option in YouTube – yet. Right now, you can only link within a video on YouTube to other pages on YouTube.

Shorter is better for video advertisements. If you decide to advertise on YouTube, 15-second digital ads are best. There is generally more inventory for shorter online ads. With voters consuming more content on mobile devices, the micro ad format tends to get more attention.

YouTube analytics

Within the *Creator Studio*, you can see top-level performance metrics for your video content. You can compare metrics for your videos to help you build a bigger audience, engage more with viewers, and create better content.

The aggregate data includes specific traffic sources from individual videos and captures data in various reports such as demographics, playbacks, traffic sources, audience retention, number of subscribers, and more.

From the **Demographics** report, you can view audience demographics like age range and gender. By adjusting the date range and geographic region, you can see how audience segments vary. That way, you can determine which audience subset views the most, and serve them accordingly.

The **Traffic Sources** report shows you how others found your videos. Viewers can find your content in many ways. These include following links from social networking sites, YouTube searches, and by clicking on Suggested Videos thumbnails. You can also see which search terms were used to find your video. (This is useful for ideas in building related content.)

The **Likes and Dislikes** report allows you to compare your specific videos metrics for likes and dislikes. Knowing what video clips are most popular may provide insight for future efforts.

From the **Audience Retention** reports you can find out which specific parts of your video clips the audience likes to watch, whether audiences watch the entirety of your video clips or just a fraction of them, and the parts in the videos where viewing drops off.

Learn which of your video clips get the most **comments**. This is a sign of community participation and can help you decide future topics of interest.

Social Video Statistics

- US adults spend an average of 1 hour, 16 minutes each day watching video on digital devices.

- 78% of people watch online videos every week, 55% watch every day.

- Facebook sees 8 billion average daily video views from 500 million users.

Source: https://www.brandwatch.com/blog/amazing-social-media-statistics-and-facts/

Online video alternatives

You might not want to use YouTube for all your video hosting needs. For one thing, you may want to have your videos display on your website without the YouTube brand and without advertising. Also, some workplaces ban YouTube from their networks. So, if an employee visits your website from work, they won't be able to access any embedded video content.

For these reasons, you may decide to split your video hosting. You could use YouTube to tap into that site's audience but use another service to provide the same embedded video content on your website.

Here are several video hosting sites, along with a brief breakdown of each service:

Wistia

https://wistia.com/

Offers both free and paid accounts. Features include adding calls to action and email capture. Free accounts include a logo on all videos.

Vimeo

https://vimeo.com

Create and share videos to groups or channels. A pro account increases your weekly upload capacity with unlimited HD uploads. It's also ad-free with advanced analytics.

SproutVideo

https://sproutvideo.com

Provides video hosting for businesses and organizations. It's worth checking out if you have large video storage needs.

Creating online video content

Internet users tend to have short attention spans. If you decide to use video, keep them short and to the point. It's better to break up long videos and group them together by topic when uploading.

Video can be recorded on everything from cell phones to digital cameras to web cams. Software to edit video ranges from free to expensive. Even after you upload your videos to some hosting services, they can still be further edited. For example, YouTube allows for video annotations as a way to add interactive commentary. You can control what the annotations say and where they appear in the video. You can also add captions and subtitles post-upload.

Online video is becoming as popular as, and in some cases, more popular than traditional political media advertising. There are instances where political advertisements rejected by 'traditional media' end up with more exposure online than if they had run on television or radio in the first place.

> Some campaign ads are purposely made excessively 'controversial' to attract more attention. They are designed to go viral, so more people see them.

Campaign videos can be used for a variety of purposes:

Personal introductions: Embedded on a website's home page, a personal introduction is a great way for voters to see and hear the candidate. A short personal message about the candidate or why he or she is running can provide depth and personality.

Campaign commercials: Convert your television and radio ads for placement on the web. Identify them by date and subject. Embed or link them into your website and post to social accounts to build interactivity.

Interviews: Videos of interviews can provide good content about the candidate. If there is no video, the audio can be put online with still images of the candidate included for the visual. If the clip is entirely audio, it is called a *podcast*.

Campaign events: Short clips of rallies, speeches, and interviews can be of interest to voters. Be sure that the clips are edited for length and clarity.

Legislative or municipal meetings: Here you can show the candidate or an opponent in action. Add annotations into the video to make specific points. Video of this type should have a purpose. For example, a video could show what a candidate says about an issue or how he or she reacts in session. You don't know a legislator until you've seen them in action.

Q&A Session: A candidate can answer voter or constituent questions in a video.

Any time a candidate is in a public setting online or offline, they should assume they are being recorded. It is standard practice for campaigns to send 'plants' to an opponent's campaign events to record the candidate and try to catch a 'gotcha' moment.

Repurposing campaign TV ads for the web

Years ago, most political consultants thought that web advertising was only good for fundraising. Nowadays, it seems that every other week some crazy or clever political ad goes viral, giving a candidate far more exposure than they could have purchased via traditional media.

If you are running TV ads, putting them online can be a great way to give your message extra exposure. An early study tested the effectiveness of re-purposed TV ads put online vs ads created specifically for the web. The results were surprising. For *brand awareness*, re-purposed TV spots and web ads performed about the same. But in terms of *conversions*, original web content performed better.

Exposure was also tested. Re-purposed ads had more effect on the viewer after four exposures. Original web content carried the most impact on the first viewing.

Ads created specifically for the web do not have to be 30 or 60 seconds long to meet television standards. Tweak your TV ads for the web to take advantage of the lack of time restrictions. Be careful, though. If a video is too long, viewers will lose interest before the benefit or call to action is communicated.

> The main call to actions for campaign communication include donate, volunteer, contact someone, forward to others and, of course, to encourage a vote.

Video recording tips

Here are some tips to make your videos appear more professional:

- If shooting with a mobile device, flip it sideways so you are shooting horizontally, not vertically. That way your video will better fit the screen or video player.
- Use proper lighting and a plain background. Make sure the lighting is front of you, not behind you.
- Use a good microphone.
- For proper picture framing, make sure there is a little room above your head.
- Take a conversational approach with your speech.
- Unless you know exactly what you want to say, consider reading from a script.
- Don't keep your head rigid. Move it a bit when you speak and look directly into the camera.
- Review and edit your material. Average attention spans continue to shrink, so the shorter the video, the better.

Unless it's a speech or presentation, aim to keep your video under two minutes.

- Embed links and use subtitles if needed.
- Consider adding a short start and end clip to each video to further brand your message.
- Get feedback from others before posting.

Again, keep your videos short and tightly edited. If you embed video into your website, *do not set them to run automatically*. Many users do not like it when a video starts playing when they arrive on a web page. They may click off immediately if they start to hear music or voices. You don't want to lose visitors that way.

When you add new videos to your accounts or website, spread the word via email, your website, and your social media accounts.

Editing your own content? <u>Camtasia</u> and <u>SRecorder</u> are popular screen recording and editing programs.

Photo Sharing Accounts

While you can upload photos to your website, there are other options available to put a social spin on them. *Photo sharing sites* allow you to share and promote content, including:

- Photos and videos from rallies and events.

- Photos and videos of candidate speeches and commercials.

- Photos from posts on other platforms (blogs, Facebook, etc.).

- Images from campaign promotional materials (yard signs, stickers, flyers, etc.).

- Images of volunteers or supporters with captions describing why they are working for or voting for the candidate.

Photo sharing helps provide transparency and gives followers an 'insiders' view of the campaign. It can help voters learn more about a candidate on a personal level, too.

When posting images to any service, be sure to add good captions and appropriate hashtags. It is easier for others to share your images when you've already provided a good context for them.

> **Photo sharing accounts aren't for everyone.** If you don't plan on maintaining photo sharing accounts, don't create them. An account that is never updated is worse than no account at all.

Instagram

Owned by Facebook, Instagram.com is a popular app for taking snapshots and short videos, manipulate and apply filters and then share them with others. Politicians use the service to reach a mobile audience.

Instagram can also be accessed on the web from a computer, but you can only upload and share photos or videos from your devices.

Every user profile has a "Followers" and "Following" count. This represents how many people they follow and how many other users follow them.

You can post both directly through the app or from existing photos/videos on your device.

Instagram Live lets people video stream directly from a mobile device. Live streams can last up to four hours and can be hosted by one or two accounts.

> 40% of U.S. adults use Instagram. *Source: Pew Research Center, 2021*

Here are some tips to help you get the most out of the platform:

Optimize your profile. That includes using your logo as your profile picture, including your website URL or Facebook link, and filling out your profile description.

Go easy on the edits. Although filter effects may be tempting, try to limit your use of them to keep the color and contrast normal in most of your photos.

Limit the text. The average view time for an image on Instagram is just three seconds. Don't place a lot of text on your images. A clever caption helps bring it together.

You can use hashtags on Instagram, just like Twitter. Create and use a few unique hashtags for your campaign. They can help others find your posts more easily.

Use the tagging feature. If someone tags you in a photo, it will end up in the 'Photos of You' section in your profile page. You can choose to hide those photos.

You can target one or more specific users by privately direct messaging them. *Instagram Direct* is a way to connect with specific groups of users.

Here are a few helpful articles to get the most from your account.

https://help.instagram.com/427910070604293/

https://blog.hootsuite.com/instagram-hacks/

https://digital-photography-school.com/10-tips-for-mastering-instagram/

Pinterest

Pinterest.com enables users to share photos, memes, and other items of interest. It's more visual than Facebook and Twitter, and is one of the most popular social networking sites in the U.S.

> Pinterest is probably not a necessary platform unless you have the resources to keep manage it.

A 'page' on Pinterest is in the format of a pushpin bulletin board. You can 'pin' videos, images and photos to your board and share them with your followers. Posted content is often liked on Facebook and Twitter.

You can sign up for Pinterest through your existing Facebook account, Twitter account, or with your email address.

Here are some tips to help you get started with the service:

Complete your profile. Fill out your profile completely to make it easier for others to find and know what your account is about. Use the profile description to indicate that the account is run by your campaign.

Connect your account. Connect your Pinterest account with Facebook and Twitter. Once you do this, you can cross-post your content.

Follow popular users. Follow your political allies and anyone who follows you first. Be sure to ask supporters to follow you as well. Follow others who repin your content. They are more likely to follow you back.

Keep it clean. Keep your pinboards neat and professional. Organize content into relevant boards and make their titles descriptive and interesting. Don't add long captions to your photos. Pinterest users are there for eye candy, not reading material.

Use #hashtags on your posts as you would in Twitter. You can also tag other Pinterest members with "@" symbol.

Use relevant descriptions. Add brief and concise pin descriptions with relevant keywords. For example, if the pin is for a fundraiser, add the candidate's name, location, and important people. Use #hashtags on your posts as you would in Twitter.

Share other user's images. Don't limit your pins to your own content. You will attract more followers if you share interesting content from other sources.

Space out your activity. It's better to pin regularly over time than in bursts of activity. Your updates are more likely to be noticed by followers if they occur more frequently.

Encourage supporters to pin and share your images whenever possible.

What can you share on Pinterest?

Opposition information

With Pinterest, political organizations can attack political opponents visually. With a little creativity, you can do so in an interesting and fun way.

Think Progress, a liberal blog, created pinboards for the 2012 presidential election. They created pinboards of *"Things Mitt Romney Would Rather Not Talk About"* and the *"Private Jets of the Romney Campaign."* This enabled Think Progress to turn campaign finance information into an effective attack.

On the Right, the *Heritage Foundation* created pinboards on topics such as *"American Leadership"* and *"On the Taxpayer Dime"*.

What is your opponent doing that you can point out in a creative way? For example, is municipal spending out of control? Use pictures to show how many X could be purchased with X amount of dollars spent on something else.

Share infographics

Infographics are an effective way to share complex data. You can find existing infographics on Pinterest as examples. Create boards for specific policies or major issues.

Campaign merchandise

Some retailers use Pinterest to sell merchandise. If your campaign is planning to sell merchandise on the web, consider incorporating Pinterest into your sales strategy.

Sample Pinterest Pages

- https://www.pinterest.com/inha/politics/
- https://www.pinterest.com/thinkprogress/
- https://www.pinterest.com/heritagefoundation/

LinkedIn

Of all the social sites discussed so far, LinkedIn.com is the least important site in relation to online campaigning. LinkedIn is a business-oriented social networking site geared toward people in professional-related fields. **It's not a site where you are likely to 'campaign', but more of a place to build your personal brand before your campaign is launched.**

To make LinkedIn worthwhile, you need an engaging, informative, and effective profile. Here are some tips to making your profile more attractive:

- **Create a clear headline.** It should state who you are, who you help, and how you help them.
- **Create a powerful summary.** Write it in the first person and in a conversational tone.
- **Use a professional photo that represents you well.** Make sure your face is big enough that it can be seen clearly.
- **If you use a personal Twitter account, connect it to LinkedIn.**
- **Create a custom URL.** Linkedin will assign your profile a random URL. Change it so it has your full name in the profile, if possible.
- **Complete the 'specialties' section**, preferably as an easy-to-skim list.
- **Complete your education and experience using relevant keywords.** Include specific detail about the kind of work you've done.
- **Spell check and proofread.** Have a few other people look over your profile for errors and mistakes.
- **Make your profile public** for all to view.
- *Selectively* **ask for recommendations** from others who can talk about specific ways you have helped them through your skills or work.

Search for others who are the top influencers in your industry. Check out how they have done their profiles for ideas.

LinkedIn Groups are sub-communities where you can take part in discussions and find contacts. Search keywords of interest such as subjects, issues, or geography to find related groups. Then request to join the group and post your questions and answers. Again, most groups (even political groups) are for discussion, not partisan campaigning.

Whether this service is something that you'll want to take advantage of is up to you. Some candidates link to their LinkedIn profile from their website. This can provide additional information or networking opportunities for those who are interested.

Social Media Don'ts

All social networks have rules to prevent spamming, user harassment, and abuse. Knowing the rules will keep you out of trouble, so you don't lose all the work that you've put into these sites.

Here are specific things that can get a candidate or campaign bounced from the major social networks (or can get an opponent bounced, as well):

Facebook

https://www.facebook.com/legal/terms

Break these rules, and you'll find your campaign banned by Facebook. Here are a few rules that can trip up campaigns and campaign staff:

Creating fake profiles or pages: While it may seem like a clever idea to create a fake parody page of your opponent, you might want to think twice. Facebook could delete everything you've created.

Posting copyrighted content: Reprinting or posting content that is not your own can get you into trouble. This can include reprinting entire news articles or copyrighted photographs without permission. You are fine if you post headlines and summaries, along with a link back to the original source.

Overtly threaten or harass others: Most things are fair game in politics, but don't use Facebook to threaten, bully, or harass your opponent or rivals. Pushing too hard can get you reported.

Posting graphic or hateful content: Enough said.

Spamming your 'friends': The line between promotion and spamming can be a fine one. Keeping your campaign top of mind should involve more than just posting fundraising solicitations. Mix up your posts. Add news, a little personal content, and human interest to keep others engaged.

Political advertising without proper authorization. This topic is discussed in more detail below.

Twitter

https://help.twitter.com/en/rules-and-policies/twitter-rules

Twitter has its own rules in place to prevent user abuse. Most of these rules are common sense, but for a political campaign it can be very tempting to bend the rules... and put your account at risk.

Creating fake accounts: Don't create an account with your opponent's name, campaign name, or organization.

Creating multiple or overlapping accounts: Don't create duplicate accounts on the same platform to exclusively cross-promote yourself or make it seem like you have an 'audience' that agrees with you.

Buying followers: Many politicians have reportedly bought followers from various services. Don't do it. Getting caught is embarrassing, and losing your account is even worse.

Spamming your followers: Not only will people stop following you if you clog up their feed with endless tweets, they may report you for spamming. If enough followers do this, you may find your account terminated.

Instagram

https://help.instagram.com/477434105621119/

Instagram terms are like Pinterest in that you are not allowed to post copyrighted images or video. Nudity and mature content are also prohibited.

Pinterest

https://policy.pinterest.com/en/terms-of-service

Many candidates use Pinterest to show and share content. The most common user violations center around the type of content posted to the site.

No fake accounts.

No posting copyrighted or hateful content: You get the idea.

Spamming: Yes, even Pinterest has issues with spammers. If you become one, your account can be deleted.

LinkedIn

https://www.linkedin.com/legal/user-agreement

LinkedIn caters to professionals who are looking to connect with others. Abusing the site can get you - yes, you guessed it – banned.

Posting copyrighted content: If you don't own the content then don't post it in its entirety without permission. This includes images and news articles. Summarize and link out to the original content.

Gaining connections inorganically: Again, spamming the network and trying to connect to unrelated people may get you banned. If you are planning to use LinkedIn, start early and build your network gradually.

Spamming forums: LinkedIn forums exist to communicate and exchange ideas. They are NOT a forum to blatantly promote your campaign or go off on political tirades. If enough people report you, you're gone.

Generally, the rules for these sites follow a familiar theme. Don't create fake accounts, don't spam, don't post copyrighted content, and don't promote hatred. If you break the rules, you can get banned. If that happens during a campaign, it can be embarrassing. Not only that, but you'll also lose a promotional forum.

And if there's one thing candidates don't want to lose, it's a promotional forum.

Dealing with negative material online

Politics - and especially local politics - can be vicious, especially on social media. And if you are a candidate, watch out!

Sure, the negative posts or comments may contain blatant lies, phony allegations, and so on. But it's important to handle these matters delicately, or else the situation can quickly spin out of control.

Most of these posts don't really influence anyone and generally make the person making the nasty post look ... well, nasty. In most cases, the material has only a small audience. They likely influence you more than anyone else.

When dealing with cyberbullies, it is best to not engage with them.

In most cases, simply ignore the posts. If a response is necessary, it's best let someone outside of your campaign or organization respond. Whatever you do, don't create new "personas" to support your position on social media, in forums or on message boards. You'll likely be caught - and that tends to make the situation worse!

Sometimes the criticism is justified

Perhaps while you posted from your mobile device, you made a misspelling or the autocorrect feature fouled up an important word. You may get called out on a mistake like this. Someone may blow your blunder out of proportion and make a big deal about it. Hyperbole often runs rampant online.

So, how should you deal with a self-inflicted wound?

Just apologize and move on. You can correct a Facebook post, but for Twitter, you'll need to either remove the original tweet or just add a comment explaining the problem.

Responding to negative posts about your campaign

If you are the person on the receiving end of criticism, it can be hard to figure out how to respond. Sometimes you'll feel that you cannot respond in a way that is acceptable to everyone or that properly addresses the issues raised.

Tips when responding to negative feedback:

- **Take your time.** You may want to lash out, but it's all too easy to make things worse if you reply while you are angry.

- **Kill them with kindness.** It's a lot easier to thank someone for their contribution than to try to debate them. Most online trolls post and move on. They probably won't even see your reply.

- **Use humor.** You may be able to disarm a troll with a witty reply. One tip is to acknowledge the criticism, apologize for it, and make light of the situation.

- **Encourage supporters to be positive and leave positive comments.** To help to combat cyber-bullying and other forms of social media harassment, try to foster a supportive community that will actively engage with others by commenting on the campaign's goals. Having people speak enthusiastically for your campaign can help it grow and develop without any negativity.

- **Hide the offensive content** and note your own online policy against such material.

As a last resort, you can report the offender. Do this as a last resort if the poster's material is especially bad. If a user breaks the terms of use of a social media service, they can be penalized. *Don't count on that happening, though.*

Should you block people on social media?

You may be tempted to block people, but you should avoid doing this. Generally, public officials should not block people unless someone is clearly abusive or engaging in hate speech. A better tactic, as mentioned above, is to hide offensive comments while noting your policy against permitting such material.

There are a lot of angry people sitting behind some keyboards.

Planning Your Social Media Updates

Most individuals (and even most businesses) do not have a clear strategy for their social media activities. Fortunately, political campaigns already have a goal in place. It is to *build exposure and attract support.*

After creating your social media accounts, the next part is determining how you will promote your campaign. How will you make sure that you are posting the right material? When should you post? How often? If you don't have a plan for how and when to post updates, now is the time to create one.

First, list the profiles and services where you post or share updates. They may include:

- Your email list
- Facebook
- Twitter
- YouTube
- Instagram
- Pinterest
- LinkedIn (professional updates)
- Text message followers
- And so on...

Next, create a checklist of all the services and profiles you post to.

This list is for you or your campaign's social media coordinator to have handy. As you get a feel for the different services, you'll find that you will want to tailor your posts for each. For example, not every tweet you make is going to be shared on every platform. You can tweet a single item several times a day on Twitter, or repeat the same thing twice on Facebook, but you should only post once on Instagram.

Have rules as to how content is shared.

Cross-posting can be effective. For example, any site updates should be shared with all accounts.

Use automation judiciously.

You may be able to set up email blasts to automatically post on Twitter and/or Facebook. Tools like Hootsuite.com allow you to manage multiple social profiles and schedule messages. Scheduling tools can work well, but each post should be tailored to the specific profile. For example, basic tweets with hashtags do not work well as Facebook posts.

> Post to each social media platform individually. For best results, craft each message to include the best practices of each service.

Several volunteers should keep an eye on breaking news.

Who is doing that and who will respond? It's a learning experience as you go along, so start early and make it a routine.

Planning ahead will streamline the process and ensure that your followers are always kept up to date.

Have a plan.

There will be many times in your campaign where you will need to get the word out quickly. Having a checklist and plan of action will help you to keep up.

See Appendix B for campaign checklists.

What is most important?

Campaigns can go deep into social media. Very deep. Large campaigns have the resources to hire staff to run, monitor, and create a multi-platform system. Smaller campaigns may have one or two people working the online side of the campaign.

The following is our action item recommendations for smaller campaigns with limited resources. How much you choose to do will depend on your comfort level, the office you are seeking, and how much you feel you need to take on.

1) Create a Google account. When you create a campaign Gmail account, it also allows you to create a Google account at the same time. A campaign Google account provides you with access to more tools, including Analytics, Google Ads, and Google Calendar.

2) Have a campaign website. A website serves several purposes. It presents information about the candidate, provides a place for online donations, and acts as the hub of your online presence. Campaign websites are discussed in more detail below.

3) Start an email list. You may think it's old-school, but email is still a great and cost-effective method to reach supporters and raise donations. Email is discussed in more detail below.

4) Create a campaign Facebook Page and Twitter account. Crosslink social media accounts with your campaign website. Update with news and information about your campaign. If you do not plan to use or update these accounts, then don't bother creating them.

5) Create other social media accounts. If you are going to use video, reserve a YouTube account. You can do this through your campaign Google account. Add relevant videos and embed them into your campaign website. Create an Instagram and/or Pinterest account if you plan to share photos.

6) Create a short message service (SMS) campaign (discussed below). Promote both online and offline wherever possible. Send alerts as necessary.

7) Engage in relevant forums.

8) Monitor your campaign and respond quickly to direct questions and comments. When engaging in dialogue, do not reply over multiple channels. For example, if you are responding to someone on Facebook, do not post the reply on Twitter.

9) Seek participation from followers rather than simply pushing out material. Ask questions. Create polls or surveys. Encourage feedback and dialogue to build and sustain interest. This can encourage others to share and perhaps even allow the material to go 'viral' and be seen by a much wider audience.

You can set up tools to automate your social media updates, but it is often better to post items separately to each platform. For example, your Tweet might be short with a hashtag, but for Facebook, your post might be longer and without hashtags.

> **Fake News?** Blindly reposting material can get you in trouble. Just because an article is posted online doesn't make it true. Far too often, politicians will share 'news' articles that are either false or written as satire. Always check your sources before you share. When in doubt, verify the facts from a reputable source.

When is the best time to post to social networks?

Besides figuring out what your campaign should post, the other question is knowing *when* to post. If you choose the wrong times, the effectiveness of your message diminishes, along with the possibility of your content going viral.

So, what do the experts say?

According to popular URL shortening service bitly.com, it turns out the best time to post depends on which social network you're posting to. Social networks have their own culture, and users tend to have distinct patterns of behavior.

One strategy is to keep 'news' type updates during the peak day times and more 'request type' posts for the evening hours.

Of course, you will want to mix things up a bit. Try some message testing and see what times work best.

Your mileage will vary, depending on your number of followers. It may be harder to test success on social networks then to test the open rate of email messages sent at different times.

No matter when you post...

Determine how much time you want to commit to social networking. You can always increase what you do, but if you start campaigning with a site or platform, you shouldn't let it wither away and abandon your followers.

As recommended at the start of this book, get to know your platforms before you start actively campaigning. That way, you are less likely to make any gaffes or mistakes.

Creating a social media schedule

Your campaign's commitment to social networking should be consistent and informative. Even if you only have a few followers to start, regularly providing interesting news, updates, and information will keep them informed and attract new followers. Putting together and following a campaign social media schedule will help keep your efforts on track.

The example below can be used as a springboard to create a schedule of your own that reflects your priorities, resources, and campaign outreach efforts.

Several Times in the Morning and Afternoon

- Check your Twitter and Facebook accounts directly or through a tool like HootSuite. Respond when necessary. Follow relevant @replies.

- Scan Twitter followers for relevant conversations to join.
- Check your campaign's email accounts and respond as necessary.
- Check your online alerts for campaign or candidate mentions. Respond as appropriate.

Weekly or on Weekends

- Add new material to your site and to file-sharing sites.
- Try to repurpose your existing content to reach a larger audience on other platforms.
- Identify new social networking influencers and build relationships where appropriate.
- Build Twitter Lists to better organize ongoing discussions and special interest groups. Set up saved searches with online tools to find out if people are talking about you or your campaign.
- Catch up on LinkedIn discussions. Send invitations to connect with influencers or important people.

Throughout the Week

- Mondays: Schedule social media. Add breaking updates as necessary.
- Participate in video conferences and meetings.
- Join conversations on social media, if appropriate. Add new content to your website and social media accounts (events, photos, news, and other items). Add images to image sites. Update other accounts, as necessary.
- Fridays: Check traffic analytics for your website and your social media platforms.

Assign staff to take on different responsibilities of your schedule. As you can see, monitoring social media can be a big job. You may want to assign several people to monitor your analytics and online mentions. Another person else might be responsible for covering events online, and so on.

If your schedule is not working, change it. Beware of committing to too much and then pulling back. It's better to start small and consistent, and then grow your efforts with your campaign.

What to do if your accounts are hacked

There is always the danger that a campaign's accounts can be hacked or taken over by a third party. This can lead to embarrassment or even the loss of a valuable communication platform.

Don't think it can happen to you? Thousands of social media accounts are hacked daily.

The key to knowing if your accounts are being tampered with is to simply pay attention to them. If you suspect that your account has been hacked, address the problem as soon as possible. Several campaign members should monitor your online presence. If anyone suspects that something is wrong, they should check with the social media administrator(s).

It's better to preemptively change a password and let everyone know afterward than to wait and see if a real problem exists.

A tip-off that your account has been hacked is when odd posts appear, unexpected notifications, or unauthorized permission or setting changes. If you notice any of these, try to log in and immediately change your password.

If you try to log in to your account and your password does not work, someone might have accessed your account and changed the password. You can try to recover your password, but odds are that the hijackers have also replaced the email address used to recover the password. In this case, contacting site support might help you get your account back.

- Google: https://www.google.com/accounts/recovery

- Twitter: https://support.twitter.com/forms/hacked

- Facebook: https://www.facebook.com/hacked

- Instagram: https://help.instagram.com/368191326593075

- Pinterest: https://help.pinterest.com/en/article/we-protected-your-account

The best defense is a good offense...

Be proactive with your social media account management and security. Here are a few tips to make it harder for others to take over your accounts:

- Use strong passwords with capitals and numbers.

- Use different passwords for all your accounts.

- Change your passwords regularly.

- Never give your username and password out to untrusted third parties.

- Make sure your computer and operating system (for you and anyone who can access the accounts) is up to date with the most recent patches, upgrades, and anti-virus software.

- Use email forwards for social media accounts. That way, you can switch where the email address is pointed to reset the account.

- Make sure everyone involved in the technical aspects of your campaign follow basic security guidelines.

Many web services are adopting two-step verification policies as a way of improving security. This "two-factor authentication" requires a user to enter a security code in addition to a password when logging in from an unrecognized device, such as another computer or mobile device. Consider adopting this verification system where possible.

How to 'fire' someone from your online campaign

The bulk of your campaign work will be performed by volunteers. This may also include your online campaign efforts. Sometimes things don't go well, and you'll find that you will need to restrict or eliminate a volunteer's access to your online accounts.

Here are the steps to take:

1. List of the accounts that the volunteer has access to. This includes social media accounts, email accounts, website logins, etc.

2. Make sure all those logins work.

3. If the user email address in the account is not controlled by the campaign, you'll need to change or disable the account's email address, so they cannot possibly retrieve their passwords via email. If an account is under their address, have them change it to a campaign email or forward address that you control first.

4. Change the passwords to those accounts. Give them to the new person or persons who will be using those accounts.

5. Inform the volunteer that you are pulling them from the accounts.

Every situation is different. The reasons why a campaign may want to revoke a volunteer's access will vary. If possible, try to 'fire' someone early in the work week. If you do it on a Friday, they might 'stew about it' over the weekend and be more likely to take retaliatory action.

While there is no guarantee that there won't be complaints or some sort of online payback for letting someone go, the important thing is the safely of your campaign accounts.

Engage your most active supporters

Many people have the potential to become strong and loyal campaign supporters. Your job is to convince them that committing to your campaign is worth their time and resources.

The early days of online campaigning were all about one-way communication. Today it is about dialogue and relationships. Your presence online will attract followers. The next step is to interact with them.

Occasionally you may find someone you do not know who posts about your campaign and actively supports you online.

Reach out to them. They may be recruited and put to more effective use. 'Virtual volunteers' can help monitor the campaign online or help spread the word through their own social media contacts. You never know what skills someone may bring to a campaign.

We discuss virtual volunteers in more detail under the Mobile Campaigning section below.

As people work for a campaign, that investment of time and energy becomes a motivation for success. Match your online volunteers to their best skills, but do not be afraid to ask more of them over time. Offline help options include putting up signs, helping with voter calling, walking the district, working the polls, hosting events, and more.

You can't run your entire campaign
from behind a screen.

Using social media at your campaign events

Social media has made it easier than ever to plan, promote, and even extend the life of any event.

Social networking can help dial up the word-of-mouth buzz before an event, virtual or in-person. Create an event on Facebook and an event hashtag on Twitter. You can even encourage people to share information about the event in return for small rewards, such as special seating or discounted admission.

Social registration services like EventBrite.com can help streamline event registration. They also allow attendees to share their event activity with friends. Some online donation services also provide event registration services.

When planning the event itself, try to create a few 'big moments' where there may be more excitement and audience engagement. If it is an in-person event, these are points when participants may want to live-tweet, make posts, or upload photos.

Promote social sharing buzz during events

- Before the event, make sure that your Wi-Fi is tested and optimized and that your displays are working. If you are live streaming the event online, conduct quality checks before you broadcast.
- Notify attendees before and during the event that they are encouraged to Tweet and post live status updates.
- Let attendees know about the event or campaign #hashtag; encourage them to use it.
- Have one or more insiders post live during the event. Mix pre-scheduled posts and live posts.
- Have someone actively monitor and respond to your social media accounts.
- Use Twitter as a real-time question collection channel.
- Ask for email addresses and Twitter IDs when people register for future contact.

Make sure you are ready to read and respond to social shares as they happen. Be on the alert for important influencers in your audience. Monitoring tools can help your volunteers track activity.

After the event, post a "wrap up" of your event's highlights. Post follow-ups to your website and social media accounts over the next few days. A successful event also provides an email broadcast opportunity.

Your Online Reputation

When voters search your name on the internet, what do they find? Are the results good, harmful, or just random? Whatever the case may be, as a political candidate, you can take control over search engine results and minimize or even eliminate unfavorable content.

Your *online reputation* is how you are perceived online. It's what people are saying about you and, perhaps more importantly, it's the information about you or your campaign that voters find online.

There are probably a few things about you right now that you don't want a voter to see. There may be negative news articles, blog posts, or comments published about you that are less than complimentary to your candidacy.

You can influence search results rather than leaving it up to chance. The most straightforward strategy is to develop new, positive information that 'pushes down' negative search results.

But sometimes your reputation is out of your control.

A few years back, we had a client who had the same name as a person who had recently committed a serious crime.

Searching Google for that candidate pulled up his campaign website - along with news articles detailing an alleged murder that 'he' committed.

Except it wasn't the candidate. It was someone else who shared the same name.

Another client shared the name of a former US President. There was no way he was ever going to get his website to appear for just a name search.

The solution?

It took some work, but both clients were able to have their information appear for name + location and name + position searches.

Sometimes that's as good as it gets.

Ways to improve your online reputation

Here are some strategies to shape your online reputation:

Have a campaign website

One of the best ways to improve your online reputation is to create a website. The best part about having your own website is that you have complete control over your messaging. For online reputation purposes, it helps if the candidate's name is included in the domain name. Top search results often include domains that contain the search phrases.

Create social media profiles

Social media profiles for Facebook, Twitter and LinkedIn often appear near the top of search results. The same goes for popular professional profile sites.

Get some coverage

News outlets rank well online. Inform the media about your campaign launch and other major events. If you can, have them include a link to your campaign website in any articles that cover the election.

Create new content about yourself

Update your website with new material. Post and share content to your social media accounts. Do online interviews, press releases, video and more to build a body of content that promotes your campaign and enhances your reputation. This is the material that will crowd out other, negative material.

Use links to build relevancy

Cross-link what you control. From your website, link out to your social media accounts, and have your social media accounts link back to your website. Linking to select outside material can also influence what appears for specific searches. Link to stories that are favorable to you and unfavorable to your opposition.

Track your online mentions

Information is power. It is important to keep up with what people are saying about you online.

Encourage key personnel to track campaign and candidate news. That includes checking your social media accounts, online news sources, and information about your opponent.

Keeping on top of what is going on is critical to managing a responsive organization. Just remember that not all news sources have a web presence, particularly local television or newspapers. They must be monitored the old-fashioned way.

Bad things can happen if no one is keeping an eye on things. Your social media profiles may attract people with malicious intent, including spammers.

Google Alerts is a service that notifies you by email when specific search terms appear on the web. To set up a notification, visit the Google Alerts submission form at https://www.google.com/alerts and type in the search term. Common searches include the name of your campaign or the candidate's name. Select "Automatic" as the source to ensure that you are notified when your search term appears anywhere online. Select 'As-it-happens' to receive the timeliest notifications. Then type in your email address and click the 'create alert' button.

You will need to verify your alert via email. Once you do that, you are all set.

When you start, you may find that your alerts are too broad and pull in too many unrelated items. If this happens, try modifying your search terms or use quotes in the search terms to limit your results, such as "TinyTown elections".

Google Alerts is sometimes slow to notify and is less reliable than it was in the past. It is better to use several services concurrently to monitor your online presence.

Paid social media tracking tools include Mention.com and SproutSocial.com.

Besides keeping tabs on your own name, be sure to monitor your opponents and news about important issues. With today's 24/7 news cycle, you never want to be caught surprised.

With some work, you can keep positive content appearing for related searches. If you can get negative material pushed down past the first page results, you've done a great job because three-quarters of people *never look past the first page of search results*.

Campaign Websites

With the rise of social media, the role of the political campaign website has shifted. Where a website used to be the bulk of a candidate's online presence, it now acts as more of an informational hub. Regardless, a website is still critical as both an online platform and as a place to reference in your advertising.

Some people confuse having a website with having an online strategy. A website is only one component of a greater online campaign. You would not pin your candidacy on having a website any more than you would on having a single tri-fold flyer or a snazzy bumper sticker. In other words, you not only need a campaign website, but also a plan to develop and market it effectively.

In this section, we will explore the creation of a campaign website – from choosing a domain name to design considerations to building out the site. You will learn what is possible, the potential pitfalls, and how to deal with all that you encounter.

Choosing and registering a domain name

Securing (registering) a domain name (i.e., smithforsenate.com) is one of the first steps you should take even if you are just considering a run for office. Registering a domain name is simple and inexpensive. You can do it long before you commit to having a website.

Domain registration and *web hosting* are two separate processes.

First, a domain must be registered through a domain registration company (called a *registrar*). That domain name is pointed to the server of a hosting company where the actual website resides. You can choose to register your domain name

89

and host your site with the same company, or you can split your domain registration and hosting between two companies.

A domain name can be registered for one year or multiple years. A few popular domain registrars include Domain.com, Godaddy.com and Name.com.

You can check if a domain name is available or not through a registrar site by performing a 'Whois' search. If the name you want is available, then you can register it for yourself.

Most registrars allow you the option of a 'private' registration. This hides the domain name owner's publicly available information and prevents the registrant's name, address, email address, and phone number from being found online. The biggest benefit to private registration is that it helps reduce spam and, increasingly, *phone solicitations*. This service adds a bit to your costs, but it is an option worth considering if you value privacy.

While it is possible to register the domain name of a political opponent, *it is not recommended*. Underhanded tricks like that are often revealed and can backfire on you. In addition, registering the name of an opponent and using it maliciously can get you into legal trouble.

On the other hand, there isn't much use in defensively purchasing every domain name that could possibly be used against you. (Such as johnsmithsucks.com) Instead, put your efforts toward promoting your own message.

In choosing a domain name, simple is best. Some political consultants advise against using your own name for a domain name. We disagree. If your name is John Smith, go with johnsmith.com or the name that will appear on the ballot. If your name is already registered, try a variation like electjohnsmith.com or votejohnsmith.com. Search engines weigh the domain name heavily in determining relevancy for a keyword phrase. In other words, if you have your name somewhere in the domain name, it boosts the chance that your site will rank well for a search of your name.

Keep the domain name short and memorable. Even though you can have over 60 characters in your domain name, how many people will want to type (or will type correctly) *electjohnsmithfortinytowncouncil.com*?

"Don't forget to visit my campaign website at vote dash smith dash for dash mayor dash of dash TinyTown dot org."

Keep in mind that domain names are *rented* from a registrar and never *owned*. You really have no control over who may later pick up your discarded domain name. For example, following the 2000 presidential election, the domain name of conservative candidate Pat Buchanan was taken over by a company whose business included helping 'swingers' to hook up online.

Not knowing who may pick up a discarded domain name is a good reason to choose a name that you will want to hang on to for a while.

Learn the fates of once-popular campaign websites at https://www.sfgate.com/entertainment/article/Click-on-a-former-candidate-s-Web-site-You-never-2640398.php

Special domain extensions

If you are looking for something a little different from the typical .com. org or .net domains, you now have more options. There are now literally dozens of new top-level domains (TLDs) available.

Want to really brand your organization? Consider registering a .democrat, .republican, .voting or .community domain.

For now, though, expect the traditional .com and .org extensions to be the norm. However, for microsites or to target specific audiences, a political domain name extension certainly draws attention.

Alternate and secondary domain names

The campaign website address of johnsmithforcouncil.com is, technically, a serviceable domain name. The problem is that long names are hard to type into a browser or fit onto campaign literature.

One way around this problem is to get a *second domain name* and *redirect* it to the original. For example, 'smith4council.com' could be pointed to the original 'johnsmithforcouncil.com' site. The shorter name is easier to use in print materials and for users to type. By using a domain redirect, you don't need to set up a new website. You are simply aliasing (forwarding) one domain name to another. That way, both domain names will continue to work going forward.

If you use a .org domain, it's a good idea to also own the .com version. People tend to type the .com domain extension by habit. If you own the .com version, you can forward it to your .org domain.

On a technical note, *domain forwarding* is referred to as a 301 redirect, with "301" interpreted by search engines as "moved permanently". It is not difficult to implement, and it should help preserve existing search engine rankings from one domain to another.

Action items

Figure out a name you want to use, along with a backup name or two in case the first is not available. If you find that the name you want is available, register it immediately. Simply searching for a domain name could trigger a domain harvester company to pick up the name automatically – with the intention of selling it to you at an inflated price. We've seen this happen to clients, and they've usually ended up having to register alternate names.

You do not need to set up a website at the time you register a domain name. At this point, you are just reserving the name and preventing anyone else from taking it. The website itself can be created later.

Domain name squatting and other dirty tricks

Domain squatting or *cybersquatting* is the term used for someone who registers a domain that infringes on another's intellectual property or trademark. Some squatters attempt to sell the names back to rightful owners for a profit. Others use them to deceive web searchers and send them to a website they were not intending to visit.

Over the years, many celebrities have recaptured their own names that were being used as domain names. In most cases, the registrant (the cyber squatter) was attempting to profit on the celebrity's fame.

But what if you're not famous (or famous enough) to argue that your own name is a trademarked term?

The *U.S. Anticybersquatting Consumer Protection Act* (ACPA) of 1999 provides protection against cybersquatting for individuals as well as owners of distinctive trademarked names. Some states have also acted. California passed the *Political Cyberfraud Abatement Act.* This act prohibits certain actions related to political domain name registration and websites.

Even with these laws, some campaigns have taken extraordinary measures to preempt potential domain squatters. The Bush campaign did this prior to the 2000 election. While George W. Bush was still governor, his campaign registered all the Bush-related names they could – including anti-Bush names such as bushsucks.com.

Dealing with domain squatters

Assuming you are not famous enough to have your name equated with a brand or trademark, you still have options available if someone registers a domain of your name. (This assumes, of course, that the registrant does not actually *share* your name.)

Go legal on them. Send a letter demanding that they cease and desist use of the domain name and to transfer all rights to the 'rightful owner'. This might scare the squatter into giving up the name. We recommend consulting with an attorney that specializes in internet law before doing this. One risk in sending a legal letter is that you may find your correspondence posted and discussed online by the other party.

Ignore the problem. Let them keep the name, while you move on and use another. Besides, 'electjohnsmith.com' should work as well as 'votejohnsmith.com'.

Occasionally, some enterprising individual may snap up a bunch of domain names related to your campaign. For example, they will offer to sell you 'votesmith.com'. But if your campaign is already using 'electsmith.com', what's the point of an additional name? If you don't want or need the name, let the squatter keep it and lose the registration fees.

Call the press. Notify the local media if an opponent has taken your name. There is no reason for a campaign to register the domain name of an opponent. After a few articles about the situation, they will likely surrender the name.

When a political campaign registers a domain of an opponent's name, they are doing it to harass the other side. Odds are, they won't create a website with it and will leave it blank with the 'default' registrar page. Using a squatted domain name to direct traffic elsewhere would cause more trouble than it is worth.

Keep an eye on any squatted domain name(s). Make sure they are never used for a website or used to redirect traffic to another website. If that happens, consider quick legal action, particularly if there is malicious or deceitful intent.

A domain scam to watch for

When your domain registration period ends, your registrar company will email you with a renewal notice. If you get a letter via snail mail... well, check it *carefully*.

If you receive a renewal notice that is not from your original registrar company, *ignore it*. Some unscrupulous companies do the phone company equivalent of 'slamming'. The scam is to have you renew your domain with the new company at a higher price than you paid with your original registrar.

If you control your own domain names, it is a good idea to occasionally log into your domain registrar account and make sure your contact information and renewal times are up to date.

Make sure that the *registrar contact* of your domain name is listed as the candidate or the campaign organization's name. *The registrar is considered the 'owner' of the domain.* It is important that the domain name list the proper registrant. That might *not* be the person who first reserved the domain.

You can check the status of any domain name through a WHOIS search. You can find this service on your registrar's site or through sites such as whois.net. Type the domain in the search box and you will see when the name is set to expire, along with other information.

Letting a domain name expire means that your campaign website and domain email accounts will stop working. The domain name will no longer point to the server where your website and email accounts reside. When a domain expires, there is generally a 30-day Redemption Period to renew. To renew during this time, the owner may be required to pay additional fees, depending on the registrar. After the Redemption Period ends, the domain will be deleted from the registry. After deletion, anyone can re-register the name and become the new legal owner.

Keep a record of your domain information. Mark your calendar for a renewal reminder at least a month ahead of time. If you renew early, the additional renewal period pushes your expiration further out from the scheduled expiration date.

Running a slate of candidates online

A multi-candidate website is a way of promoting several candidates in one place. Usually, the candidates are all from the same party or they side together on a major campaign issue. They become a 'slate' of candidates, hoping to win an election together as a block.

While there may be efficiency in a multi-candidate online campaign, there are also drawbacks to the strategy.

The Positives

- **A multi-candidate website works best for issue-based or grassroots campaigns.** It can be used to introduce the candidates and lead voters to related online material.

- **Slate sites can work for local political parties where all the candidates share a general platform.** A slate site often includes candidate bios and may link out to individual websites.

- **It is easier to promote a single site as a focal point for advertising and online fundraising.** Obviously, it costs less to build and maintain a single site than multiple sites.

The Negatives

- **It may be difficult for voters to square the candidates' differing views on issues.** This assumes that the candidates 'share' the issue pages. In our experience, it is unlikely that all candidates will agree on every issue position.

- **If candidates are fundraising for themselves, collecting donations through a shared site can be tricky.** If one or two candidates are more successful, they may overshadow the others.

- **Getting initial content and update approvals can prove difficult.** If a site is 'run by committee', requiring every candidate to provide approval before any content changes can be made, then nothing will get updated – or it won't get updated quickly.

Running a slate of candidates does not mean that all or none will win. We have seen instances where half the slate has won, and half did not. Particularly in local elections, success often comes down to how well specific candidates manage their campaigns and get out the vote.

Ultimately, each candidate wins or loses on his or her own merits. Whether a slate of candidates should combine online efforts or not depends on the circumstances. How the candidates run together should be worked out well in advance.

Action Items

If you plan to have a website with multiple candidates, take time to figure out how the site will be structured. Will every candidate have their own bio page and share the issue pages? Or will each candidate have their own issue pages? What makes them a slate? Is it an issue? A political party? Usually, a slate website has a unifying theme.

If a slate site for unrelated candidates is used just to save money... well, voters will probably pick up on that.

No one's ever picked up votes by being frugal.

Using microsites to extend reach

A microsite is a small, self-contained, single-issue website. They are designed to promote a specific issue or idea. They are useful when you want people to focus and act on a specific topic. For example, a microsite can be used to educate voters about a specific new law or local development. They can also highlight an opponent's position or weakness. ("Who's making political contributions to ...")

Best of all, microsites tend to become viral. They may get shared with others, particularly if the site has a humorous or clever spin.

Another advantage of microsites is that they keep negative information off your own website while giving you the benefit of an attack from elsewhere.

A recent trend in political attack microsites is to have the site appear to be 'independent' or not affiliated to another political campaign. Independence tends to lend credibility, even when it might not be deserved.

Even more cunning is the use of 'independent' blogs or websites to circulate information that is simply not true. With today's never-ending news cycle, we find that rumors, innuendo, and outright false information are often picked up and passed along as breaking news without verification. *Corrections* never seem to get the same coverage.

Here are some topic ideas for starting a political microsite:

- **To expose corrupt practices.** You can highlight an opponent's corrupt actions or conflicts of interest. Use featured videos and content to hammer home your points.

- **Highlight a specific issue.** This may be an expansion of an existing campaign issue. With a microsite, you can go into more detail and target support for that issue. It can also be used to fight back against something that is supported by an opponent.

- **To point out an opponent's lack of work ethic.** During the 2008 US presidential election, a microsite named WheresLiddy.com was created to track Elizabeth Dole's travels outside the state. The point of the site was to show how she was out of touch with her constituents.

- **Donor details.** Use a microsite to point out exactly who is donating to your opponent – and why. This is effective if you can tie together legislation and/or conflicts of interest between your opponent and their donor(s).

- **To set the record straight.** Here, the microsite can be designed to refute false claims against a candidate. It can also be used as an 'attack' site to lay out facts against an opponent.

- **To play games.** With a large enough budget and a little creativity, you can create an online game poking fun at an opponent. Players can rack up points by adding up your opponent's campaign contributions or trying to choose which positions your opponents have taken on issues. (Surprise! Your opponent has been quoted as taking both sides on *every* issue!)

Again, a microsite can be separate from your primary campaign website. You may want to promote the microsite from your main site or let it stand alone. Plot out your goals, come up with a great domain name, and create the content *before* you build out the site.

In the next section, we explain how to do this.

Planning Your Campaign Website

Content is king on the web. Because of this, we are starting this section with a discussion about the text and image elements that comprise a website. Planning your content ahead of time makes building your site much easier.

Preparing your content

When you strip away the bells and whistles, a website comes down to text and visuals. A typical political campaign website has, but is not limited to, the following content:

Home Page: The home page can be used to announce the campaign, why the candidate is running, and what the candidate hopes to accomplish. In time, this text can be updated to include new developments or to shift focus from awareness to support gathering.

Biography/Resume: Start with some basic personal information, such as family, time lived in the area, hobbies, etc. Take your resume and work it into a short biography. Keep it short and bullet-pointed, but don't simply make it a list of your work or political history. Work in a few words about what you did in those positions and how they may relate to public service. Your bio should tell more than just whether you are qualified. It should also give reasons for voters to relate to you.

Issues/Positions: This is the heart of your website. Issues can be split into separate pages or combined into one page. Stake your positions against those of your opponent. If you have a large amount of detailed material, break it out further, perhaps into downloadable files for easier reading.

Endorsements: Include organizations and direct quotes, where possible. Endorsement quotes should be added throughout your site, particularly where they are relevant to specific issues.

Voter Registration Information: Provide a summary of local voting requirements. Provide links to your state and county voting registration information.

News/Updates: Often referred to as a 'blog', this part of the site can include announcements, links to news, and event coverage. To start, this section can contain an initial press release announcing your campaign. Additional material can be added over time.

Events Calendar: This can be set up as a list or a calendar of upcoming events.

Contact Page: A basic form is often included on the contact page. Unless it is necessary, do not require a large amount of information from users to submit a form. A name, an email address, and a phone number should be enough.

Donation Page: This page can be used to accept online donations and/or tell people where they can send money. The page can have a donation form or link out to a secure donation page elsewhere. Be sure that your donation page requests all the donor information required by law.

Volunteer Page: This page can include a form to gather information from those who want to help the campaign. Include a list of recommended activities for volunteers to select in the signup form. These may include:

- Displaying a yard sign
- Running errands
- Hosting an event or fundraiser
- Sending postcards to friends
- Walking and door knocking in the district
- Phoning voters
- Raising contributions
- Getting out the vote
- Being a poll worker

You may want to keep the information request from potential volunteers short. Name, phone number, and email are good. Additional information can be gathered during the follow-up conversation. You may also want to ask whether the volunteer wishes to have their name used in the campaign.

Press Kit: This page can provide digital versions of campaign literature, images, and other information about a candidate and the campaign.

Privacy Policy: Most people don't read "legalese", but a good privacy policy helps build trust, particularly with potential donors. It's best to be restrictive with your privacy policy and promise not to sell or share visitor information. Privacy and terms of use generation is discussed below.

Disclaimer: Most municipalities require by law a disclaimer as to who funded the site or campaign treasurer information. These disclaimers are typically located in the site footer.

Action Items

As you put together the basic content structure of the site, list the pages and features that you would like to include in your campaign website.

A website is an organic thing. It grows and evolves over time. Don't worry if you don't know everything you want the site to initially contain or exactly how you want it to look. It's always a work in progress.

Writing for the Web

The internet provides political campaigns with a cost-effective method to communicate with voters. However, writing for the web is different from writing for print. Simply copying your campaign print material onto your campaign website limits the potential of this medium.

Studies show that people read from computer screens about 25% slower than they read from paper. Most readers scan website text rather than carefully reading it. They look for relevant terms and navigate accordingly.

Nobody likes scrolling through pages and pages of poorly written, overblown website copy. Give your visitors the information they need – and make it interesting. Create content that is exclusive to the website and remind visitors to return frequently.

Use these tips to make your content more readable:

- Put the main points of your document in the first paragraph.
- Write concisely and stick to one idea per paragraph.
- Use lists and bullet points rather than wordy sentences or paragraphs. Readers can pick out information more easily from a list than from paragraphs.
- Use meaningful sub-headings. Guide the reader by highlighting the main points.
- **Bold your main points**.
- Separate longer policy information and link out to it for readers who want to know more about a particular subject. PDF files work well because they can be easily printed out for offline reading.

Putting it in the right tense

Sometimes candidates are concerned that their website is not ranking for search results as well as it should. This usually has to do with the age of the site, existing content that already ranks for the targeted search phrase, and whether the website content *mentions the name of the candidate.*

Believe it or not, there are campaign websites out there that barely mention the candidate's name. Sometimes this is due to the *tense* in which the content is written, and it can make all the difference to a search engine.

Writing in the *first-person* narrative means writing from the "I" point of view. Such as: *I am running for office. I have the necessary skills and ability to do the job. My background is in...*

The *third person* form is to write from the omniscient point of view. Such as: *Bob Smith is running for office. Bob Smith has necessary skills and ability to do the job. Smith's background is in...*

See the difference?

Writing in the first person is:

- More personal sounding
- Replaces the candidate's name with 'I'
- Tends to become stilted and boring in delivery
- Can hurt search engine rankings if the candidate's name is never mentioned

Writing in the third person is:

- More authoritative
- Allows more 'branding' by mentioning the candidate's name more often
- Generally better for search engine ranking

A search engine cannot know what a web page is about if there isn't enough relevant text on the page.

We recommend that you write your web content in the third person, using the candidate's full name when relevant. Writing in the third person tends to be less repetitive and provides an edge in search rankings.

First person narrative is often more appropriate for a candidate's personal message or an 'open letter to voters.' If you use this type of copy, add 'pull quotes' on the page that mention the candidate's name. A pull quote is a brief quotation or phrase pulled from the main text and added as a separate blurb.

Don't forget these!

You would be surprised how frequently crucial information is *left out* of campaign websites. Here is information that every campaign website should include:

State/Municipality/Office Sought: It's amazing how many local campaign websites say, 'Candidate X for Mayor', but don't mention the municipality's state. If you are running for office in Montgomery, is that Montgomery, New York or Montgomery, Alabama? Don't make us guess.

Primary/General Election Date: Don't assume that everyone knows the day they need to go out and vote for you. Add the year, as well. A lot of old websites are out there still asking for votes, even though Election Day has long since come and gone. It's another good reason to keep your website up-to-date, even after the campaign.

Specific Phrasing for Local Issues: The more local the campaign, the more specific the issues become. Don't just say 'our traffic problems', say 'TinyTown's traffic problems'. Again, this helps your site rank on the search results related searches and may attract more visitors.

Contact Information: Provide full contact information for your campaign. This will be helpful to both voters and the media. After all, if they can't easily contact you when you're running for office, why should they assume you will be more responsive when you're elected?

Use direct-marketing writing techniques

Does your website (and print) copy persuade people to react to your campaign? Use these direct-marketing techniques to improve your content effectiveness:

Use powerful subject lines: Subject lines should be compelling, as they are the most important part of your copy. A good subject line should grab a reader's attention and make them want to continue reading.

Write in the active voice: A sentence is said to be in active voice when the subject of a sentence performs the action of the verb. Changing how you write a sentence can increase its effectiveness. For example, 'The dog bit the mailman' is better than 'the mailman was bitten by the dog.'

Sell yourself: Tell your visitors how they will directly benefit if they support your campaign.

Make calls to action: Prompt your reader to act. Tell them exactly what you want them to do: Donate, join the campaign, subscribe to your email list, forward along a web page, etc. Don't assume that anyone knows what you want from them. Spell it out.

Keep your content up to date: Make sure your website is regularly updated. Use 'teasers' on the home page and put your full updates on your news page, calendar page, or blog. Keep your content fresh and people will have a reason to keep coming back to your site.

Optimizing your web content (SEO)

You can optimize your website content to help your web pages rank better on search engines for relevant searches. This is called *search engine optimization*, or SEO.

These tips will help optimize your writing so search engines can more easily find and index your content.

When you refer to your important keyword phrases, do not truncate them. For example, write, 'John Smith has a history of public service,' not 'Smith has a history of public service.' This helps raise the relevance of the candidate's name as a keyword associated with the website. The same idea applies with using your hometown, the specific office sought ("Mayor of TinyTown") and other important phrases. *Consistency builds relevance for search engines.*

Include the main keyword phrases early in your text and use them in headings to break up your content. Search engines assume that the most important search keywords appear near the top of the page. This includes the headline and the first few paragraphs of text.

> "Do you know where to hide a dead body? It's on the second page of Google because nobody goes there!" - Miles Anthony Smith

Too much of a good thing?

Search engines can penalize a website or even exclude it from appearing if they detect search engine 'spamming.' An example of this is repeating a word or phrase over and over on a page to increase search engine rankings. Write your content for readability and this shouldn't be a problem.

With a little optimization and links from outside sources like your campaign social media accounts, your site should rank well for relevant searches. Times vary, but it can take anywhere from a few days to a few weeks to see your website appear in search engine results.

Essential website disclaimers

All US jurisdictions have laws covering the use of disclosure statements on political advertising. Items that typically require a disclosure statement include billboards, bumper stickers, sample ballots, newspaper ads, TV and radio ads, magazines, mass mailings, websites – and even email.

The specific wording required is usually some variant of "*Paid for and authorized by*" the candidate or political group. Adding a disclaimer to a campaign website is simple. Most campaigns typically place this information in the footer of each web page.

Besides the "Paid for" disclaimer, consider adding these additional disclaimers to your website:

Privacy Policy: It's best to be restrictive with your privacy policy and promise not to sell or share visitor information with anyone. This section can also cover users under a certain age.

Terms of Use: Sometimes these are lumped together with the privacy policy. Other times they are broken out. Your terms of use may cover a variety of situations. Your terms of use should address the following:

- Disclaimers: This may include that the website is provided 'as-is', privacy notification, and provisions specifying information which needs to be disclosed.
- Limitations: Limiting liability for any user damages.
- Revisions: That the material on the site may not be accurate and subject to updates.
- Links: That you are not liable for any content on outside websites, and that there is no endorsement implied.
- Governing law: Of the appropriate state.

We recommend that you get legal advice to make sure that your policies are valid. There are online web policy generators that can help draft your site disclaimers. They include:

FreePrivacyPolicy.com

https://www.freeprivacypolicy.com/free-privacy-policy-generator.php

Privacy Policy Generator

https://www.bennadel.com/coldfusion/privacy-policy-generator.htm

PrivacyPolicyOnline.com Terms of Service Generator

http://www.privacypolicyonline.com/terms-of-service-generator/

Website Content Preparation

Users make decisions about the quality of a web page by the way it looks. A great design is critical for making a positive impression. Having an idea of what you want your website to look like makes the design process go smoother.

Design elements to consider

Candidate photo: This is the most common feature in a campaign site header. Perhaps it's the nature of politics, but we have never encountered a candidate who did not want their photo front and center on their website. The best shots for designers to work with are those with the subject in front of a solid color. This makes it easier to crop and edit the image.

Colors and fonts: The colors of the header (and website) should be consistent with the color scheme of your other campaign material. Political colors do not have to be limited to the traditional red and blue (in the US). Be sure the site colors and logo match your print materials. Consistency builds familiarity.

Location: It's great that your website is all about 'Smith for Mayor', but mayor of where? Never assume a visitor knows where you are located. Display your municipality and location in the header.

Slogan or quote: This is optional, but if you have a great campaign slogan, why hide it?

Landmarks: Identifiable natural or man-made landmarks make for a great header background.

Header sizes vary. When we started designing political websites in the early 2000s, most website headers were narrow. In time, they became taller, with room enough to include a candidate's full shoulders and chest. These days, narrow headers consisting of a logo and navigation are more common. Larger "hero images" are often set below the navigation. Styles change continually, even on the web.

Site footers come in all sorts of designs and colors. Common footer items include disclosure statements, terms of use, privacy, and contact links.

To give your designer an idea of what you are looking for, put together a brief list of sites that you find attractive. Note the design elements that you like. Providing this sort of information up front can help get your initial design mockup completed faster – and have the result look more the way you envision it.

Putting your content together

Web designers often encounter clients who do not provide the necessary content to build out their website. One way to save time (and money) when getting your website built is to organize your content ahead of time. This makes it easier for the designer or developer to put everything together properly.

When the body copy, page title, meta tags, and images are already prepared, you are more likely to have your site built the way you want. It will be better optimized for search engines from the start.

A dirty little secret of web designers is that if you don't tell them what to use for page titles and meta tags, they often stick in generic text for them – or none at all.

What are meta tags?

While you are writing your initial site content, you should include meta tag information for each page. The title and description are the two important tags that search engines look for when indexing website content.

The *title tag* or page title specifies the title of a web page. The title tag should be a concise description of a page's content. Title tags are displayed on search engines as the clickable headline for a given result. They also appear as the title in web browsers.

The *description meta tag* is a short snippet of 160 to 180 characters. Search engines often use a web page's description meta tag as the description for search results. This is simply a descriptive sentence that describes the page.

You can see how it works with this works with this simple HTML page code:

```
<head>
<title>John Smith will fix TinyTown traffic</title>
<meta name="description" content="Candidate for Mayor
John Smith vows to take on the traffic problem in
TinyTown.">
</head>
<body>
<h1>TinyTown Traffic is Terrible</h1>
<p>On November 2, vote for John Smith for Mayor of
TinyTown. He's ready to tackle the traffic in TinyTown!</p>
<p>Tied up in endless traffic? It's time for the town to install
new traffic lights!</p>
<p>And this is the third paragraph.</p>
<p>And so forth...</p>
</body>
</html>
```

Below is a sample page of website content. If you can provide this kind of information to your designer before they start working, you'll be ahead of the game. You will see that there is no HTML or coding. That is something the designer would create when the site is built, in addition to placing images or graphics.

Your initial page content can be saved as a Word document or even as text files. The information would be sent to a designer or developer along with all your high-res images.

Sample content notes for a designer:

File Name: tinytown-traffic.html
Page Title: John Smith will fix TinyTown traffic
Description: John Smith vows to take on the traffic in TinyTown. Vote for Smith on November 8th!
Images for page:

- *candidateheadshot1.jpg (place near top of page)*

- *traffic-light.gif (place halfway down page)*

Body Copy:
TinyTown Traffic is Terrible

On November 2, vote for John Smith for Mayor of TinyTown. He's ready to tackle the traffic in TinyTown!

Tied up in traffic? No wonder! Mayor Bill Smith has ignored the problem for three years. It's time for [new traffic lights] (link to https://mynewspaper.com/tinytown-traffic-lights.html) and updated signs. We want to keep our streets safe for all TinyTown residents...

Preparing graphics and images

From brochures to websites to press releases, photography plays a key role in any political campaign. We live in a visual world, so a campaign's images need to be compelling and help tell a story to voters. Having a good stock of visuals at hand will make it easier to create quality promotional material.

A good photographer is a great investment. Quality photography pays dividends in your campaign's overall impression and professionalism.

Candidate head shots

Your candidate head shot is one of the most important pictures you will have. There will probably be one image used repeatedly throughout the campaign. Take several sets with different outfits. If you are wearing a formal outfit, try taking some pictures without a jacket. Wear solid colors rather than patterns and stripes. Have your picture taken against a contrasting neutral background. This allows the background to be more easily cropped out.

Head shot tips:

- A head-on or three-quarter view is typical.

- Make sure BOTH shoulders can be seen in these shots. Don't crop them off!

- Dress appropriately.

- Smile!

Example of a good candidate head shot with shoulders and a background that can be easily cropped.
Source: Library of Congress (loc.gov).

Family photos

Though family members may not be directly involved in your political campaign, family photos are an important way to give voters more idea about your life and story. These can be staged in your home or in outdoor settings. The candidate should be front and center. You might want to avoid vacation shots or anything too out of the ordinary.

Informal photos

These can be taken both indoors and outdoors. They can show you in a variety of activities. They don't all have to be 'happy'. For example, you can show the candidate in his or her work setting, getting the job done. Get some non-staged pictures from campaign events or just slice-of-life in daily activity. The best photos are those that appear spontaneous.

Different groups and audiences

Show yourself engaged with others, rather than simply posing with people. They can include senior citizens, youth or students, veterans, work organizations or other groups. Focus on voter groups or organizations that the campaign is specifically targeting. These types of photographs show that you have a relationship with that segment of the electorate.

Make sure you are not overdressed or under-dressed in comparison to your audience. Some photos should be 'candid' shots that look like they might have been taken by nearly participant.

Photos with notable people and endorsers

A photo with a prominent endorser can improve your reputation and show that you have a relationship with notable people. Group table or side-by-side event pictures are good, but photos of the subjects interacting or speaking together are particularly powerful.

Other photo ideas include posing with staff and volunteers. These types of pictures show staff appreciation, boost morale and are great for posting to social media. If someone who is voting for you wants a picture with you, go for it. Make sure you ask for and have permission to use the image later.

Pictures with local landmarks and locations

Get photographed in locations that voters can identify. They can include local neighborhoods, schools, parks, waterfront, or major landmarks. Dress appropriately for the location. For example, a subject should be dressed more casually in a park or natural setting. Be sure to get any required permissions for your locations.

Take extra photos of the landmarks alone. They can be used for other design purposes, such as watermark images, as part of website/social media headers or reference shots in print material.

Think wide! Consider how a photo might look as an edge-to-edge image on a website. Take some wide panorama shots with every set of pictures you take.

Panoramic shot of Market Square in Washington, DC.
Source: Library of Congress (loc.gov).

Photos on .gov websites are considered public domain. If you need a photo of a public figure or building, you can always pull official photos from a .gov website. (Your tax dollars at work!)

Photo Release Forms: Anyone who is photographed for a campaign should sign a photo release. This includes parents or guardians of children. If you are taking photos of a group event, make sure that the people are made aware. This helps protects the campaign legally and prevents unnecessary surprises.

If you are doing your own image work, there are online tools for resizing and compressing graphic files. They include pixlr.com, lunapic.com and fotoflexer.com.

Professional graphics software includes Photoshop, Illustrator, and CorelDraw.

For a less-expensive alternative, consider Photopea. It is a web-based graphics editor that can work with raster and vector graphics. It has similar in features to Photoshop. There is a free and paid version.

Always save backups of your original uncompressed graphic files and photographs. Once an image is compressed by being saved as a JPEG or GIF file, data is lost, and you cannot recover it from that image file.

Looking for an online graphics solution? Canva.com is a graphic design platform that allows users to create social media graphics, presentations, brochures, and other visual content. It is available on web and mobile, and integrates images, fonts, templates, and illustrations.

Action Items

If someone is building out your website, the process will go smoother if you prepare each page of your content in a standard format. Include titles, meta tags, text, images to be added to the page, and any other details a designer might need to know.

Remember to keep backups of all your original images.

Brochures and other content to share

When building your website content, it's a good idea to separate your longer policy information and link out to it for readers who want to know more detail about a particular subject. Some people want to know the basics of where a candidate stands. Others want detail. By supplying the most information, you satisfy both types of voters.

PDF files work well for supplying compiled information. They can be printed out for offline reading. PDFs can also be sent as attachments or linked to within email messages.

PDF stands for *Portable Document Format*. To view and print a PDF file requires a download and installation of the Adobe Acrobat Reader. Most computers have Acrobat Reader software already installed.

Consider converting your campaign flyers, handouts, and brochures into PDFs. That way, you can save money and have supporters share and print materials. Put your entire media kit online for download.

PrimoPDF is a free online PDF creator. This service allows you to generate PDF files from Word and Excel documents. You can even create snapshots of web pages. A paid version of the software lets you mark up your files, create PDF forms, and more.

Newer versions of Microsoft Word and Excel let you save files directly to a PDF format.

Where to share

You can always upload content to your campaign website. If you have large files or want to keep them elsewhere for public consumption, there are other places you can upload them.

Social publishing websites allow users to upload PDFs, Word, and PowerPoint documents for others to read and share. From these sites, anyone can embed these documents within web pages, allowing the material to go viral.

These sites are recommended for storing and sharing files. The last two allow for a link back to your website in the 'About' area.

- docs.google.com - If you have a Google account, you can access Google Drive to store and share files.
- Slideshare.net (owned by Scribd)
- SpeakerDeck.com

You can upload position papers, brochures, PowerPoint, Word files, and other documents. Then you can embed those items back into your campaign website. Keeping documents in a central location can be convenient in case you need to revise and replace them.

Online press releases

Press releases are an excellent way to promote yourself and your campaign. A press release is a short, newsworthy article about your campaign that is distributed to relevant media contacts. There are differences between offline and online press releases.

Before you create a press release, you should have something newsworthy to publish. Each press release should focus on a single story or issue, such as:

- Entry into a political race.

- Upcoming event or fundraiser.
- Key endorsements.
- News related to the campaign.
- Policy statements.
- Reaction to event or opponent's action.

Your release should have a precise and interesting title and subtitle of about a dozen words or less. Where possible, include relevant keyword phrases, such as location and the office you are running for.

The first paragraph should sum up the release's content and delve a bit into the meat of the story. Start with an attention-grabbing fact. Keep your sentences and paragraphs short. Try to work relevant keyword phrases in your text, while still maintaining a readable text flow.

Go into more detail throughout the main body of the release, expanding on the initial opening paragraph. Include research or statistics from credible sources. Keep the tone businesslike and write in the active voice. Don't include personal or unrelated details.

The closing paragraph should repeat the main point of the release. It should direct the reader to where they can go for more information. Include a contact name, email address, website, and contact numbers.

Keep your press releases to a maximum of 300-500 words — and be sure to proofread them.

Besides posting press releases to your website, you can *syndicate* them. This means submitting your press release to one or more *press release websites*. Including a website link in a release can build links to your site from the sites where your release is published. Releases from press release websites can also appear in search results. Very rarely, however, do online releases attract real media attention.

Press release websites that allow for a live link in the release include OnlinePRNews.com, and PRLog.org. Smaller press release sites often copy content from larger ones.

Once a press release has gone live, *promote the version posted on your website* through your social media accounts. You could promote releases posted offsite, but why send people elsewhere?

The strategy of syndicating press releases is less useful than it was in the past, as Google no longer ranks press release content as well as it used to. However, online press release can still help new sites trigger search engine indexing of a website.

Who Will Build Your Site – And How?

A well-designed web site instills trust and confidence. It can make your organization appear larger than it really is.

In this section, we will explore the process of finding a website designer or design firm to build your campaign website. For simplicity, we will refer to anyone who is a website designer, website developer, or programmer as a *web designer.*

Before you look for someone to design your website, you will want an idea of what your project will entail. If you followed the steps in the previous chapter, then you should already have your basic requirements, initial content, and primary images ready.

You may find that an eager designer will volunteer to build your campaign website. They may support you politically, but it is also possible that they are looking to use your site as a future portfolio piece. While there is nothing wrong with that, a campaign website is an expression of a candidate. An unattractive or amateur design will not project a professional image. Your campaign website should not be someone's school project or resume sample.

At the same time, *free website builders* suffer from the same problem. It can be tough for an amateur to make those sites look good.

You want to project a professional image. This is the main reason why a professional design is worth the added cost.

Every web designer or design firm has their own strengths and weaknesses. Some firms specialize in political websites that incorporate built-in features such as volunteer and donation forms. They often have fixed prices for their services and a fast turnaround time. They may also offer extra services, such as integrated fundraising systems or graphic design.

Whether you go with an independent designer, a design firm, or a political website service, you'll need to evaluate your needs against their services, work practices, and prices to determine what will work best for you.

Content management systems

A *content management system* (CMS) allows you to update your own website. You may have heard of *WordPress* and *Joomla* as popular examples. A CMS exists as a way of separating design from content. A designer creates the visual elements. This includes the site header, navigation, sidebars, etc. From there, users (or the client) can add, edit, and delete specific pages and content without effecting the overall look or flow of the website.

A CMS can increase site flexibility while reducing time and costs spent on site management. It becomes obvious when you compare the cost of having a CMS website vs. the costs of a website built 'by hand' and paying a developer to make updates. Most websites today incorporate some sort of CMS.

Before you commit to a particular CMS, you should become familiar with how it works. Ease of use and functionality are what separates one CMS from another. Do not assume that a CMS necessarily equals 'simple to use'. Some are difficult to master. There will likely be a learning curve, no matter the system.

The cost of content management systems varies. Many of them, such as WordPress, Joomla and Drupal are *open source*, which means you do not have to pay to use the software. The costs come from the setup, configuration, and design customization.

Pricing your project

So, what should a campaign website cost to create? That's a good question with a complicated answer.

Prices can vary widely. Building a website requires time, technical knowledge, and design skills. Your specific website requirements and budget also play a factor in pricing.

You can always build your own site, but what is your time worth? If you are a candidate, your time is probably better spent performing campaign activities, rather than learning technical skills and coding.

So, what will cost? Again, it depends.

Here are some *very* rough pricing estimates for a small (5 to 15 page) website with a custom design and some sort of CMS so you can update the site going forward:

Large web design firms cost more than small firms or solo designers. Large firms have a greater overhead and often have a minimum project size. Expect to be quoted prices in the thousands, even for a simple website.

Small firms or solo designers will likely charge anywhere between $500 to $1,500 dollars and up for a basic website. Quality and cost can very between designers. Support levels can vary as well, particularly for solo designers who build websites as a 'side job'.

Paid website builders range in price from $15-$50 per month. For the most part, you are designing your own site with online tools. Features related to political campaigns may be limited. As noted above, free packages may have domain transfer restrictions or display advertising on your site. Some builders have package or service upsells.

Many factors can influence a project price. For example, is the designer familiar with the needs of political organizations, such as donation functionality? If not, they may want to create an expensive custom donation solution rather than integrating a more cost-effective existing service. Selling items through your website (ecommerce) will substantially increase your price. Need custom programming? That will also cost you.

It's complicated pricing out a website project. Knowing your requirements and having content ready ahead of time is a big help.

Choosing a web designer

Selecting a web designer may seem to be a daunting task. Designers range from individual freelancers to large media agencies. Do you want to work with someone local that you can meet face-to-face? Or are you comfortable dealing with people over the phone and via email? Do you want to work with a designer who specializes in political candidate websites? Will a 'website package' with a set number of features work for you, or do you need a truly custom solution?

A few searches on the web will provide you with all sorts of designers and design firms. Visit their sites and get an idea of the type and scope of business they do. Look at their online portfolio. You may be able to find reviews and client testimonials on other, unrelated websites. Try searching for the firm or site name + 'reviews' or 'testimonials'.

Narrow down your options to several designers. Then call them and ask some questions. Get a feel for how they communicate and if they seem to be a good 'fit' for your project. This will narrow your selection further.

Here are some questions to ask when speaking with a designer or design firm:

Do they charge by the hour – and is there a cap?

Without a time estimate, a website project can easily end up costing more than expected. Request a flat fee for the entire project, or if you are paying by the hour, request a fee cap.

What is the turnaround time?

This cuts both ways. A designer is dependent on a client providing materials on time so they can create proofs and build the site. Having your material ready at the start will speed up the initial design process. Be prepared to quickly review drafts and answer your designer's questions.

Will there be a custom design?

Some designers work from pre-designed templates. While this is not a bad thing, you may find the designs are not as professional or look more 'cookie-cutter'. On the other hand, there is time and cost savings associated with using templates. The designer's portfolio should give you an idea of the variety of their work.

What CMS will be used?

Most website designers have a CMS that they favor. It's likely that if you work with a particular designer, your CMS is already decided. They may be able to show you a demo of how it works.

A note on templates: A CMS allows you to edit the website content. A template within a CMS provides the 'design' aspects of the website. You can change a site template or edit some template elements within a CMS, but for a truly custom design, you will likely need the skills of a web designer.

Who will do site updates?

This is where the 'gotchas' come into play. If your site is built with a CMS, there is no reason why you should not have access to log in and make updates or additions to your site.

You should never put your web presence at the mercy of an outsider. Political campaigns cannot wait two business days to respond to events. In an emergency, someone from the campaign needs site access to make fast updates.

If you pay an outsider to make site changes, how much will updates cost you? Many designers charge a 15-minute minimum. If you bombard a designer with multiple changes, your costs will rapidly add up.

Our advice is to have a professional create your campaign website but leaves you in control to make future updates.

How will the site be optimized for search engines?

Your CMS and the pages it renders should incorporate good SEO practices. This includes having unique page titles, description meta tags, and proper coding techniques. You can control a lot of this by organizing your own content before the project.

Will the site work for mobile users?

A *responsive website* renders well on desktop computers, mobile phones, and tablets. Mobile internet usage is now greater than desktop internet usage. Your website must provide a great user-experience across different devices and screen sizes. If your designer cannot create a responsive website for you *or wants to charge you extra for that functionality*, find someone else.

Will the site include an SSL certificate?

SSL (Secure Socket Layer) is the standard security technology for the web. An SSL certificate activates the "padlock" icon for a website in a browser's address bar. It changes the URL to 'https://". This shows that the connection is encrypted for security. With the ever-increasing importance of online privacy, SSL helps increase visitor trust by encrypting communication between the visitor and the website. This includes any personal information sent for donation purposes.

Does the price include a domain name and hosting?

Often domain names and web hosting are add-ons to a design project. If you need a domain name and website hosting, make sure this is included in the project. Sometimes this may be a separate expense if the designer arranges hosting through a third party. Domain names are registered for an annual period, so that tends to be a fixed recurring cost.

Are there any guarantees?

If your designer is unable to complete the project, will you be able to get some or all your money back? Most designers will not return an initial deposit after they have created a site mockup. This is to prevent a client from taking the initial designs and having someone else complete the work.

References

Besides checking online reviews, you may want to reach out to previous clients from your selected designers. Ask if they were happy with their service. Find out if the project was completed on time. If any problems occurred, how were they handled? Most importantly, ask if they would hire that designer or firm again.

If the references are not particularly good, consider going with someone else. Trust your instincts.

Make the plunge

Once you have selected a designer, you may need to sign an agreement and pay a deposit. Most designers have standard agreements. Read them carefully and be sure that each required element of your project is included. Be sure the timescale and payment terms are clearly spelled out. There should also be specifications as to how project alterations will be dealt with in terms of cost and delays, and how any disputes that may arise will be settled.

Ambiguity often leads to problems, so be sure to ask and get answers to any questions you have *before* you make the commitment.

If all is well, sign the contract (or make the order in the case of a service) and get that site built!

Unabashed plug: OnlineCandidate.com provides affordable campaign website packages specifically designed for political candidates. The system has built-in tools and can fully integrate with other web services, such as email and online donation vendors.

What To Know About Website Hosting

A web host is a company that maintains specialized computers called servers that store a website's files and make them available to others through the internet. If you are hiring a web designer to build your site, they will typically arrange for hosting and will include those costs in your project.

Many domain registrars offer inexpensive website hosting. Basic web hosting can range from $10 to $250 per month. The high end is for dedicated servers hosting for very large websites.

Free website hosting is not a good idea. You may be forced to display outside ads on your website. The web host may have little customer support, and they may close shop without warning. This is one case where you definitely 'get what you pay for'.

Below are some issues to consider when determining hosting needs:

Disk space: Disk space is like space on your computer's hard drive. It is calculated in a similar format – in kilobytes, megabytes, and gigabytes. A website's required disk space is determined by adding up the size of all the website files, including the image and multimedia files. Unless video or audio files are stored on your host server, it is unlikely that your website will use a large amount of disk space.

Bandwidth: Bandwidth is the amount of overall data sent by your hosting server to people accessing your website. It also includes outgoing and incoming email traffic. It is generally offered in gigabytes/month.

Most web hosts will not host video files, due to the potential for excessive bandwidth use. A list of video hosting services can be found in Appendix A.

If you have a bandwidth cap, you can reduce your site's bandwidth usage in two ways. One way is to make sure that all your site images are optimized. This means resizing their physical dimensions and saving them in the proper file type.

> **Tech Tip:** Website images that are the correct size and saved in compressed formats will both reduce bandwidth and help web pages load faster for users.

Email options: Some things to look for are the number of email aliases or forwarding addresses provided, mailbox storage size, online email access, and spam filtering. Email is discussed in more detail below.

Hosting support: Most web hosts offer free email support. Some also offer phone support, which may involve additional charges.

If your website developer is providing web hosting services, will they be available for support? If the site goes down unexpectedly, will they be able to restore it again quickly?

Changing website hosting

At some point, you may need to move your website from one website host to another. Your current designer may not be in the hosting business anymore (or suddenly not available), or you may be redesigning your site and want to start over with a different web host.

Moving a site will involve a DNS (domain name server) change in your domain registrar account to point your domain name to another server. *Before* you make that change, make sure that the entire content of your old website – the pages, images, databases, and scripts are first copied over to the new location and are working. If your site is based on a CMS, then that software will need to be set up again and configured.

If the page file names of the old site and the new site are not identical, you will want to set up proper *301 redirects*. The redirects will help preserve the search engine rankings of your pages.

Only after the new site is set up and the necessary redirects are in place should the DNS change be made. Once the switch is made, incoming traffic will go to the new site. There may be some back and forth between the old and new site as the DNS changes propagate through the web. This may last for a day or so.

A final word

Website hosting is usually the last thing people think of when getting a website created. If the hosting is reliable and fast, that is all that matters.

Problems tend to occur when site owners want to change hosts. When that happens, find a skilled developer who can migrate your website with minimal site interruption or downtime.

Setting Up Search Engine Accounts

Search engine accounts provide many useful tools and services. They are an important step in getting your site indexed by the major search engines. You can create search engine accounts well before you have a website to submit.

Google Account

https://www.google.com/accounts/

As discussed previously, creating a Google Account for your campaign is highly recommended. Many campaigns create a campaign Gmail account to get started. Accounts are free and allow you access to several useful services, including Google Ads, Google Alerts, Google Analytics, and more.

The *Google Search Console* provides detailed information about your site's visibility on Google, what other sites link to your website, opportunities to diagnose site issues, and to see how visitors arrive at your site.

Add your site to the Google Search Console at

https://search.google.com/search-console/about

Bing Webmaster Tools

https://www.bing.com/toolbox/webmaster

Microsoft's Bing search engine is number two in overall search engine volume. A Bing account provides a means to directly submit your site through *Bing Webmaster Tools*, and to get information on indexed pages of your site, links to your site, and specific keyword performance.

Due to a Bing/Yahoo arrangement in 2010, the old *Yahoo! Site Explorer* merged into Bing Webmaster Tools.

Verifying your website

Once you have set up your search engine accounts, adding your website is simple. What can get a little tricky, though, is the *verification* process. (The search engines want to make sure that whoever is submitting the site controls it.)

To verify your site ownership, you can upload a small, named file to your website root directory. You can also add a meta tag to your home page header code. Or, in the case of Google, have *Google Analytics* already installed and verified. (Website analytics is discussed in the next section.)

These steps should be simple for any web designer.

Once the verification step is complete, you can confirm ownership. Your search engine accounts will soon provide information about your website status, backlinks, and more.

Measuring Website Traffic

Knowing what resonates with voters and supporters is important in maintaining a successful online presence. While you can track some activity through social media accounts, you still want to know what visitors do on your campaign website. How many people visit the site? What pages do they visit? On what pages to they enter or leave your website?

To track on-site activity and interaction, you will need to set up *website analytics.*

Many web hosting companies include built-in traffic statistics programs, such as *Webalizer* or *AWStats*. They use server log data to provide basic website usage information, such as the number of site visitors and where they came from. Large organizations use higher-end analytic programs like Adobe Analytics. Most local campaigns have neither the budget nor the technical expertise to set up complicated analytics systems.

But if you really want to know what drives traffic and what people are doing on your site, there is another solution – and it's free.

Google Analytics

https://analytics.google.com

Google Analytics is a web analytics solution that gives you insights into your website traffic and marketing effectiveness. It is easy to set up and install. To start, you need a Google Account. You must sign into your Google account or create a new account if you do not have one.

Once you have added your site and answered a few questions, Google Analytics will provide you with a block of *tracking code*. Copy and paste this HTML code directly into each page of your site.

That's it. You now have basic website tracking.

What can analytics tell you?

Generally, there are two basic questions that require answers:

1) Where do your visitors come from?

The '*Acquisition > Overview*' section displays the sources which send traffic to your website. This can be broken down further into:

- **Organic Search:** This is the number of visitors who came to the website by searching through a search engine. Note that most of the actual keywords used to find your website will not be shown.

- **Direct Traffic:** This is the number of visitors who came to the website by entering a URL into their web browser (or are unable to be tracked in other ways).

- **Referrals:** Referring websites are sites that send visitors to your campaign website.

- **Paid Search:** This includes traffic from pay per click advertising such as Google Ads or Bing Advertising.

- **Social:** This is traffic from known social networking websites.

You can drill down further into each report to find additional information about each of these channels.

2) What are your visitors doing on the website?

Analysis of this data enables you to track visitor's actions on the website. You can find out what pages were looked at, for how long, and whether they were the first or last pages a visitor saw. The '*Behavior*' section of Google Analytics provides this data.

- **All Pages:** This contains a list of the most popular content as viewed by visitors.

- **Landing Pages:** This lists the pages where your visitors first arrive. You can examine the browsing path for each webpage to determine traffic patterns.

- **Exit Pages:** This contains a list of pages that led visitors to exit the website.

Note that in these reports, the '**Bounce Rate**' listed is the percentage of visitors that landed on a particular page and immediately left the site. A high bounce rate indicates that visitors may not be finding that content engaging. Those pages may require content improvement.

More advanced users can track how visitors get to certain pages like the volunteer signup form or donation page. To do that, you will need to create goals and funnels. The '*Goals*' category helps you to set a goal or goal path. By segmenting traffic, you can find out how many visitors completed or did not complete your goals, the overall value of your goals, and what sources of traffic performed best.

Tracking ad results

With Google Analytics you can keep track of your advertising sources and activity on your website. All you need to do is add parameters to the links of your ads. The parameters include:

Campaign Source: This is the website or e-mail list where the visitor sees your ad.

Campaign Medium: What type of ad is it? It could be a banner ad, a Pay Per Click ad, or an email link.

Campaign Name: This is the specific promotion of the ad. For example, it could be "BBQ Fundraiser" or "Get Out the Vote".

Campaign Term: This can be used to identify paid keywords.

Campaign Content: This is used to differentiate ads, such as by design or slogan.

Google URL Builder

With the Google URL Builder you can insert advertising values into your individual advertising links:

https://ga-dev-tools.appspot.com/campaign-url-builder/

Here is an example of a URL edited for tracking. Using the parameters listed above we transform a landing page link:

https://www.yourcampaignwebsite.com/donate.html

into

https://www.yourcampaignwebsite.com/donate.html?utm_ source=DonorList&utm_ medium=Email&utm_ campaign=G OTV&utm_content=Last%20Chance

Note: The question mark separates the base URL from the special parameters. The *"%20"* characters signify a blank space.

When you use tagged URLs in your ads, Google Analytics will be able to track the link activity and actions. You can track results through the *'Acquisitions>Campaigns'* section in your account.

By tracking your online advertising, you can determine how certain ads perform and which ads or channels resonate best. This will help you budget your online advertising efforts and improve your messaging.

Action Items

Before your campaign site goes live, determine how you are going to track your site traffic. Consider using Google Analytics because it is simple to install and powerful. If you tag your online advertising, you can see how each of your ads perform.

Building Website Traffic and Support

'If you build a website, they will come' is a common belief held by many new to the web. However, the reality is that people will not come to your campaign website unless you promote it both online and offline.

In this section, we will look at maintaining your web presence, building website traffic, online fundraising, and recruiting volunteers.

Maintaining your web presence

Once your campaign website is up and running, the work has just begun. Your website is more than a digital pamphlet. It should be an online hub and a place that voters can visit for updates, news, and information.

Depending on your level of technical expertise, you may want to handle website updates yourself, or you may want to assign the duty to others in your campaign. Many campaigns have a volunteer who acts as a *website coordinator*.

Some web designers or hosting companies offer *website maintenance packages*. That is where you pay a flat rate for a set amount of site update time each month. You may find this to be an attractive option, but be aware of two things: First, things move fast in a campaign, so how quickly will they make requested changes or updates? Two, will *all changes* have to go through them? If your site is set up through a content management system, then anyone with proper access can update it. There should be no need to have updates bottled up through one outside person or service.

A website coordinator can perform many duties, including:

- Posting site updates.
- Managing social network profiles.

- Responding to voter emails and social media correspondence.

- Composing and sending e-newsletters.

- Coordinating online fundraising campaigns.

- Managing online volunteer offers.

- Handling online advertising campaigns.

Set up a system to make sure that your website, email, and social media needs are in place. Web coordinators should work closely with the rest of your campaign staff. They must also be able to act quickly and have enough leeway to handle routine matters themselves. Lay out your expectations early and set up specific guidelines for any staff involved in your online campaign.

Political campaign blogging

A blog (short for 'web log'), is a website or a part of a website that is updated frequently with news, commentary, articles, and more. New items, called posts, appear on the top of the blog's main page with older items underneath.

Blog functionality is built into many content management systems, such as WordPress.

Blogging provides an easy way to maintain up-to-the-minute updates. A blog post can quickly make a campaign's message public. Quick response to real or perceived problems enhances a campaign's image and reputation.

Any campaign can benefit from having an ongoing blog – the key word being ongoing. If a blog is set up and nothing is posted to it, it is worse than not having one at all. Don't add a blog section to your website unless there are plans for it to be regularly updated. In time, visitors might wonder if your campaign is still active.

Campaign blogging tips

- Keep your blog posts relatively short, around 300-500 words.

- Stick to a regular publishing schedule. Little and often is better than a lot and then nothing for several weeks. If you are looking to build ongoing interest, consistent updates are the key.

- Incorporate photos into your posts.

- Use titles that are descriptive of content.

- Don't plagiarize. If a local newspaper writes an article about your campaign, paraphrase, possibly editorialize, and then link out to the original article. If you want to copy an entire article in a blog post or news item, make sure you obtain permission first.

- Remember that what you post on a blog becomes part of the public record.

- Refrain from posting a link to any material that has not been read through thoroughly and carefully.

- Update previous entries as new material becomes available.

- Correct any errors and omissions promptly.

Turn the comments off on your blog. For a political campaign, it is your forum, your message. You will want to keep it that way.

Creating an online political press kit

How does an online press kit work? Unlike a physical press kit, an online press kit is designed to be downloaded in part or whole. PDFs work well as a common file format for most documents.

An online campaign press kit can include:

- A cover letter describing the candidate and campaign.

- An official candidate biography.

- Press releases in file form.

- Digital copies of logos, brochures, flyers, and any other print materials.

- Photographs of the candidate and campaign events. Consider offering several versions for download. Low-res files can be used for web, but print requires larger, high-resolution images for decent results.

- Newspaper or other media excerpts. Rather than reprinting the material outright, you could create a document or PDF file with links.

- A Question-and-Answer sheet covering the major issues. This could include standard platform information and cover basic questions about the candidate.

Avoid fluff about how great the candidate is in your material. Keep your information professional and up to date.

You can convert files and documents into PDFs through free tools like primopdf.com or dopdf.com. Images can be grouped together and compressed into ZIP files. WinZip is a popular compression program, but there are free alternatives available such as JZIP.

Reach out to the media early. Find out which reporters cover your area. Send them a quick introduction and contact information, letting them know where to access your online press kit. Anything that makes a journalist's job easier can only help improve the coverage of your campaign.

Squeeze pages

In the world of online marketing, a squeeze page is a single web page designed with the purpose of capturing information. Squeeze pages use *direct response marketing techniques*. That includes the use of headlines, bullets, teaser copy, deadlines, incentives, and testimonials. These elements are designed to influence the visitor to buy, subscribe, or sign up for more information.

What works for businesses can also work for political marketing. Here are the basic components of a squeeze page:

- Intriguing headline
- Explanation
- Request – and who is making it
- Bullets listing why the person should act
- Request for action
- Reassurance

As an example, let's write out a candidate contribution squeeze page. The bracketed text would be edited with specific information related to the campaign.

++

Show [Opponent] Just How Strong We Are

Last week, [Opponent] voted to [do something terrible that hurt the community]. Now the people of [Location] are saddled with [something awful]. Let's show [him/her] in [November] that we won't take this lying down!
- [Candidate Name for Position]

Help me inform voters about who [Opponent] really is. We have a responsibility to push back against [Opponent] because his long pattern of behavior [contradicts his campaign message].

- [Opponent] has raised over [$$$] this campaign cycle.

149

- [Opponent] supports [legislation to kick puppies].

- [Opponent's legislative agenda] can only be stopped by bringing [his/her] actions to light.

- [Candidate] will fight back and bring [positive change] to [Location].

- With Election Day only [two weeks] away, we have little time to waste!

Contribute $10, $25, $50 or $100 to my campaign by clicking the button below. Every contribution makes a difference!

Your information is secure. Federal law requires us to use our best efforts to collect and report the name, address, occupation, and name of employer of individuals whose contributions exceed [$$$] per election cycle. Contributions or gifts to [Candidate] are not tax deductible.

++

With a little work and some persuasive copywriting techniques, you can turn squeeze pages into powerful tools. Use them as landing pages for your online advertising.

For best results, limit extraneous elements from the pages. Additional links or graphics can distract a reader from your message and cause them to click away. This is a reason why you might want to make your landing pages separate and different from regular pages on your website.

> **TIP:** The squeeze page writing format works well for email messages. It helps keep your messaging focused.

Linking Techniques

Links are the currency of the internet. Reciprocal linking between related sites not only increases potential traffic, but it helps improve search engine rankings for relevant searches.

Below are ways to increase traffic and search engine prominence through building links to and from your website and social media accounts.

Authoritative linking

Your content appears stronger when it's backed up by creditable sources. This includes online newspapers, magazine articles, or links from organizations.

When writing about an event, link directly from the text to the original online source(s). Not everyone will check sources. For those that do check, they will find proof behind your statements. That will give greater weight to the rest of what you have to say.

When creating a link to source material, link the phrase *within* your text, rather than breaking it out by using a 'click here' link. Format the links to open in a new browser window. That way you won't completely lose readers if they follow outside links.

Well-cited, rational content will win out over opinionated rants any day.

Related sites and blogs

Are there local or regional web sites that would agree to link to your site? What about other local candidates and organizations? Are there county and state political blogs that would link to your site? Ask other groups campaigning for similar causes to put a link from their website to yours and offer to do the same for them. Consider reaching out to like-minded websites. By trading links, you can both benefit from the cross-traffic and bring exposure to others interested in similar issues.

With a little work, you can help boost your search engine rankings and attract additional visitors who may be interested in your campaign.

To find relevant sites, run a search for 'political blogs' and your region or state. Sites related to a campaign issue may also yield results. Once you've found sites you want to engage with, reach out to them.

Linking out to a site is a great way to get their attention and provides a great opening when contacting them. "Thanks for the article on XYZ. I linked to it from my campaign site at..." Getting to know other site owners this way may help improve coverage and give you the opportunity to suggest story or post ideas that could help increase your campaign's exposure.

Another idea is to offer to do an email or podcast interview. You can do this either as questions you answer via email or as a series of contributed articles or recorded podcasts. In any case, you'll want to have the material you contribute link back to your site.

Site owners typically follow related sites. Once something about your campaign appears on one site, do not be surprised if others start reaching out to you.

Viral marketing

'Viral marketing' refers to the online phenomenon of people sharing information with other people, who in turn share it with others, and so on. Viral marketing can be very powerful.

Online viral marketing techniques include:

- **Social Sharing:** Links that allow visitors to share, bookmark, and save pages and content.

- **Email newsletters:** Encourage viral marketing by asking recipients to forward your newsletters to others.

- **Email signature:** Most email programs allow you to create a 'signature' that is added to the bottom of every outgoing personal email message. Make sure your campaign staff's email accounts contain a campaign signature.

- **Image or video:** Video has become one of the largest segments of social media. Investing in video and video promotion can pay big dividends in traffic and exposure.

- And, of course, **traditional social media channels** such as Facebook, Twitter and Instagram are the primary sources of viral content on the web.

Opponent links

Ask sites that link to your opponent to link to your site. For example, newspapers will often put election information online. If they don't have your website address, you are missing potential exposure.

To find out which sites are linking to your opponent, visit Google.com and enter your opponent's domain name (no www). This will show web pages that mention and link to your opponent's website. Run the same test on your own website. Sometimes you will be surprised by who links to whom.

Submitting to search engines

Finally, here is something you *don't* have to do.

If you have already created search engine accounts and have a few links back to your website, your job is done. Even if you do not create search engine accounts, websites usually become listed without any effort on the owner's part. They are picked up by software 'spiders' (also called 'bots') that crawl the Web looking for new or changed web pages to add to their indexes.

> **WARNING:** Avoid paid services that offer to submit your website to a bunch of search engines and directories. They are a waste of money. You may get offers for these services when your register a domain name without adding a privacy option that hides your personal information.

Offline promotional materials

It's probably obvious, but don't forget to include your website domain on promotional material distributed by your campaign — fliers, press releases, posters, banners, bumper stickers, TV, and radio ads. Some political consultants don't believe in putting a domain name on yard signs, but that's up to you.

Online Communication Tools

Besides a source for websites and social media, the web can also serve as an internal communication tool for political campaigns. Cloud-based (another word for Web-based) applications can help improve group workflow and collaboration.

There are many cloud-based communication applications. Their services vary in functionality. Selecting one or more is a matter of preference. Features and pricing change rapidly in this evolving market, so here is an overview of a few popular services.

> **There is a lot of overlap in tool functionality.** Some services provide a while array of features, while other services are more limited in what they do. Smaller campaigns may want to stick with basic file sharing, project management, and video content platforms. Larger campaigns may want to invest in full-blown customer relationship manager services.

File sharing services

A single place for campaign staff to access documents can make life easier for everyone. Until recently, the only way to share electronic documents was to email them or store them on a website. Both methods can be insecure, and neither allow for easy collaboration.

Google Docs

https://www.google.com/docs/about/

This is one of the best-known document sharing services. It has a simple interface and offers office apps for creating documents, spreadsheets, presentations, and forms. It accepts popular file formats such as DOC, XLS, RTF, CSV, PPT and more. Users can collaborate with others in real-time on the same documents. Combined with the services of Gmail, Chat, and Google Calendar, it can become a campaign's all-in-one internal communications tool. There are both free and paid versions.

Google Docs is a good choice, as you may already have a campaign Google or Gmail account.

Dropbox

dropbox.com/

Dropbox allows users to save files to their computers, phones, and the Dropbox website. Shared folders allow users to work together on the same projects and documents. Files are accessible by installing Dropbox software on every user's computer or device. There is both a free and paid business version.

Microsoft Office Web Apps

products.office.com/en-us/free-office-online-for-the-web

A free cloud version of Microsoft Office Web Apps exists for Office. It offers a way to access, view, and edit Word, Excel, PowerPoint, and OneNote documents directly from your browser. Personal Office Web Apps on the cloud-based SkyDrive are available for free. For collaborative use, *the service is fee-based* and requires Office to be installed on each user's computer.

If members of your campaign organization are web-savvy, consider using online tools to share and update data. It's safer than emailing documents or uploading files to a website directory.

Project management platforms

As you piece together your online components, you may find that you need a way to communicate with other team members beyond email and file sharing applications. To keep in touch on a project level, consider using an online communication platform. Here are a few services that can help keep your online goals on track.

Basecamp

basecamp.com

Basecamp is group communication tool for desktop and mobile devices. Where other services allow you to integrate third-party services, many of those tools are already built into Basecamp.

As an organizing tool, Basecamp helps you track priorities and actionable items. You can create to-do lists, schedule, assign tasks, and set due dates. Conversations can be shared with everyone or with selected individuals. Integrated real-time group chat allows for direct messaging between individuals. Basecamp will even follow up on overdue tasks.

Outside emails can be forwarded directly into Basecamp. This helps organize email chains and notifications. Every project includes space for documents, files, and images. You can share to-dos, messages, and files with others, including outside vendors. Everything is private unless you choose to share.

Basecamp offers a free trial. There is a single price for unlimited projects and users. If you are planning on using multiple communication tools, you may find it more affordable and efficient to just use Basecamp.

Slack

slack.com

Slack is an internal messaging and communication tool designed for project teams. It is designed to replace email as a primary communication method. The app allows managers to organize and focus conversations, set reminders, and track operations from a single centralized platform.

Communication can be organized into private channels. Group by team, project or whatever else is relevant to your organization. For example, you can create separate channels for field operations, fundraising and communication. Team members can be added to channels that are relevant to their role(s). Private channels can restrict sensitive communication to relevant team members.

Slack helps eliminate redundant email chains by centralizing communications. It can replace email, text messaging, and instant messaging within teams.

Slack integrates with third-party services, such as Google Drive, Dropbox and more. It also has a mobile app so users can keep in touch on the go.

Outside campaign vendors can be added to specific channels for external communication. Anyone can be removed if they are no longer affiliated with the campaign.

Slack is free to start for an unlimited number of users.

Trello

trello.com

Trello is more of a project management app than a communication tool. It can help manage specific projects and keep them on track. It's easy to use, even for less technically savvy users. It can be accessed through a desktop computer or mobile app.

Trello uses "Cards" and "Boards" as a digital form of post-it notes. The cards and boards are used to organize projects. Each card includes comments, uploaded attachments, checklists, due dates, and more. You can assign tasks and priorities and move specific projects from start to completion.

The platform integrates with apps like Google's G Suite, Evernote, and Slack.

Free to start, Trello lets you can have unlimited users/team members collaborating on a board. Larger organizations can upgrade for more security features and additional integrations.

Video conferencing services

Looking to connect with your team online? Video conferencing allows you to hold real-time meetings with others who are in different places.

Not long ago, video calls and conferencing required expensive equipment and expertise. Today, you can host or participate in video conferencing sessions on mobile devices as well as desktop computers. Meetings can be set up easily and quickly.

Some video conferencing services include:

- GoToMeeting.com
- Google Hangouts (limited participants)
- Skype (limited participants)
- Webex.com
- Zoom.us

> Zoom.us became popular for its ease of use during the pandemic in 2020. Zoom integrates with many platforms and services, including *Slack* and *Trello*. Personal accounts are free. There is a paid version for teams.

These services include the ability to host online events, so they can be used for more than just campaign staff communication. You may need to upgrade to a paid account to access the full range of features.

You can always use more than one tool to get the job done. But if you plan to host campaign fundraisers or larger group meetings, consider using a paid service that can accommodate those expanded needs.

Contact Relationship Managers

It's important that your campaign can maintain a good relationship with your voters, supporters, and volunteers. While many campaigns and organizations use spreadsheets and documents to keep things in order, a Contact Relationship Management (CRM) provides an efficient way to organize, communicate and build your network.

Most CRMs are specialized for business, where the 'C' in 'CRM' stands for Customer. Some CRMs are designed specifically for political campaigns and nonprofit organizations. Many allow integration with popular online tools.

Whether you use a CRM or not is up to you. Many campaigns do fine keeping track of information with documents and spreadsheets.

Here are a few popular services, in alphabetical order:

Everyaction

everyaction.com

(For Democratic or progressive organizations.) Easily build, customize, and embed donation forms. Create emails with a drag and drop editor. Manage events from start to finish, including online forms and integrated fundraising. Influence decision makers with one-click advocacy actions and use secondary asks to turn advocates into donors. Includes analytics tools to track progress and evaluate your campaigns.

FundHero

fundhero.io

Fundhero is donation system combined with a CRM. Set up multiple or single donation pages with multiple templates. Keep track of conversations, pledges, donations, and next steps. Create easy to pull, premade financial reports. Donor profiles allow you to track conversations with supporters.

Hubspot

hubspot.com

Hubspot is a popular CRM and marketing platform. It provides ways to capture, track, and grow leads. It includes hundreds of integrations, so you can connect with other services you may use. Other features include integration of Live Chat and Chatbots into your website. Hubspot offers a free version of their software, with the ability to upgrade for additional marketing tools.

Pipedrive

pipedrive.com

Track calls, emails, and contact history. It includes a scheduler and activity calendar. It also easily integrates with other services and tools, including text and phone platforms. This CRM can be useful for local and state-level campaigns.

Salsa Labs

salsalabs.com

Provides donor management, fundraising, advocacy, event, and marketing automation tools. Salsa Engage Petitions allow you to rally active supporters and gain new ones around a specific issue. Organizations can use text-to-initiate and broadcast features to grow their list and reach out to supporters. With full social media integration, organizations can post directly from within the system.

If you plan to organize your staff or keep in touch with supporters online, consider using a CRM rather than cobbling together separate tools. The CRM market changes quickly with new services and consolidation. Each service has its strengths and weaknesses. If you think you want to use a CRM, take the time find one that best suits your purposes.

See Appendix A for a full list of online communication services.

Political Fundraising Online

The most effective way for local campaigns to raise money is still the 'old-fashioned' way — by making calls and holding events. Personal contacts and solicitation are still an integral part of the fundraising process.

Online fundraising can be a great way to bring in campaign funds. It can help you target a wider audience and tap into a greater quantity of small donations. People who hesitate to write a check might be more inclined to contribute online.

As technical barriers have dropped, virtually all political campaigns now raise money online.

Opening a political campaign bank account

A bank checking account serves several purposes. It allows you to accept political donations and contributions from supporters, and by using your account you can easily make campaign purchases.

Open your campaign checking account as early as possible. Campaign finance laws in many states require that a campaign bank account be established to legally deposit political donations. The sooner you have an account, the sooner you can start raising money.

Prior to opening an account, you may need to establish a political campaign committee with your local county Board of Elections. The name you use for your campaign committee is the name you will use to open the bank account. The bank will require committee paperwork along with personal identification.

Open an interest-free checking account rather than an interest-bearing savings account. Any interest earned on a campaign bank account must be reported in your finance reports. Considering how little banks pay in interest, the small amount of money to be gained is hardly worth the additional reporting required by your committee treasurer.

A candidate's personal funds can be used for campaign purchases before a campaign bank account is established. Those purchases are generally treated as an in-kind donation or as a personal loan. Once the campaign is underway, the treasurer should handle the political funds and keep track of income and expenditures. For larger campaigns, it may be a good idea to hire an accountant.

Keep detailed records of every account transaction for financial filing requirements. Statements, records, and receipts (paper and electronic) should be stored in a safe place. They should be held indefinitely in case questions later arise as to your campaign finances.

As always, be sure to know and follow your local election finance laws to the letter.

Anatomy of an online donation

Under no circumstances will the internet magically bring in money. Your online campaign presence exists as a conduit through which to raise money, not as a means unto itself. If your campaign is not well promoted or no one has an interest in your campaign, slapping up online donation buttons will not do a thing for you.

On the other hand, online fundraising can be very successful if done properly.

Accepting online donations carries associated costs. Services that allow you to accept online credit card contributions charge transaction fees (typically between 3 – 5%) that are deducted off the top of any payment. Some services also charge setup and recurring fees. Regardless of how you raise money, your campaign must follow the law. For example, you may need to collect certain donor information or there may be a legal limit on contributions.

> **Check your local laws for donation requirements.** If necessary, seek legal advice for any fundraising plans you have.

Below is a summary of a typical payment process for online donations:

- After clicking a 'Donate Now' button or link, visitors enter their billing and other requested information on a donation or contribution form. Then they submit their information to start the payment process.

- After submission, a payment gateway takes over. A payment gateway is a service process that verifies and electronically moves funds. The donor's credit card is electronically verified and charged. Then the funds are deposited into a Merchant Account. This account may be in your organization's name or in the name of the payment gateway vendor.

- When the transaction is complete, the donor is shown a confirmation page and sent an email confirmation. At this point, a record of the transaction becomes available for your campaign's reporting purposes — and the donation process is complete.

Online fundraising and donation services

Payments online can be accepted either through a *third-party processor* or through an *online merchant account* requiring a bank partner. Merchant accounts require more resources to manage and are suitable only for large organizations. Either way, if you decide to pursue online donations, you will need a campaign bank account and verification of your organization's non-profit status.

Third party processors

Third party payment processors (or "aggregators") provide a simple and inexpensive way to accept payments online without the expense and obligation of owning a merchant account.

Pros:

- Fast implementation.
- Built-in tools for tracking, integrations.
- Requires little technical knowledge to set up.
- Generally, no setup or recurring fees.
- Low transaction fees – typically 3-5%.

Cons:

- The vendor's name, as opposed to your campaign's name, may appear on the donor's credit card statement.
- You may not be able to access your money right away if there is a holding period.

Once you have been approved and paid any applicable setup fees, you can create embeddable donation forms, links, and 'Donate Now' buttons. These forms, links and buttons lead to the third-party processor's website or app, where they process donations on your behalf.

After a donor contributes, the funds are credited to your account, minus the processor's commission or fees.

Political-based processors have integrated systems for adding events, selling tickets, and tracking donations. They also make it easier to comply with Federal or state donor requirements. Some services cater specifically to Democratic or Republican candidates.

Using a politically focused third-party processor is advised.

Some campaigns still use PayPal to collect secure donations. While the fees are low, PayPal lacks many features that political-based processors have, including donor information recording and social media tools.

See Appendix A for a list of online fundraising services.

Crowdfunding initial support

Crowdfunding has become popular a popular tool for raising early money. It works in a similar way as donation services described above but focuses on small donors to fund a specific goal.

For local campaigns, crowdfunding can provide a jump-start to the initial fundraising process. It can help candidates who cannot afford to self-fund their campaign launch. It offers a way to test the level of support and secure initial pledges *before* establishing a formal campaign. It's like a 'conditional' fundraising campaign.

There are numerous services that operate as crowdfunding sites. Each service is somewhat different. For example, GoFundMe.com is used more for nonprofit organizations and causes.

Crowdfunding offers a way to quickly get the ball rolling and establish pledges of support before making a commitment to run. Early success sends a signal to other potential donors that the campaign is viable.

For candidates looking to have some financial backing before diving into a candidacy, crowdfunding offers an alternative to traditional fundraising.

Comparing costs between fundraising systems

Suppose one online fundraising processor service has a 3% transaction fee. The second has a 6% transaction fee. Which service will leave your campaign with the most money? The first, right? After all, it takes a smaller bite out of every donation, right?

Unfortunately, the math isn't quite that simple...

Say the 3% service is bare bones and allows you to add a button to your campaign website and a contribution link for your email. Let's say you bring in $10,000 in donations. After expenses, you are left with $9,700.

Using the 6% service is more expensive. It leaves your campaign with $9,300 after deducting costs.

But suppose the higher-cost service has additional tools to facilitate online fundraising. Let us say that in addition to buttons and email links, the 6% service provides custom contribution pages, social media widgets, and online viral tools. Suppose that extra functionality helps bring in *just 10% more* in donations.

That extra 10% would provide an additional $1,000, for a total of $11,000. After taking away the 6% fees, you are left with $10,340. That is $1,040 or *11.2% more money* in your coffers than the 3% service brought in.

If you can leverage the tools of the 6% service to bring in 20% more, then you could bring in an additional $1,980 or 21% more money.

Keep in mind that the scenario above is an example, and results can and will vary. Your fundraising success will not only depend on your payment processor, but also how you use your online tools, the size of your campaign, and other factors.

If you decide to use an online fundraising service with more bells and whistles, plan to *use* those bells and whistles to get the most from your efforts.

> Frugality is not a virtue in politics. Trying to raise and spend as little as possible is a sure way to electoral defeat.

Put your pieces in place

When you are ready to start, you will need to sign up with a fundraising platform and have your account approved. Before your start your accepting online donations, you should have in place:

- **A campaign bank account** – You will need a bank account to deposit your donations.

- **A website** – This is the place to send supporters and where to point online advertising.

- **An email marketing tool** – Such as MailChimp or Aweber. More extensive options may contain a CRM to track donors and supporters.

- **Social media accounts** – Use Facebook and Twitter to keep supporters in the loop.

- **A Google account** – For setting up your campaign Gmail and website analytics.

- **A press release** describing your goal.

The best way to start marketing your fundraising initiative is by launching a website. A simple site where you can host your donation form is sufficient to start. Make sure everything is working properly before starting any promotion.

Your online pitch

Website donation pages typically start with a few short sentences about how and why a donor's gift will make a difference. There is no need to go into detail about your campaign. At no point should the donor be distracted with other links or information about other giving opportunities.

Your donation page should also note any legal requirements that your campaign may fall under, such as:

- That no corporate funds may be used for a contribution.
- That the donor must be a citizen or resident alien.
- That the donor does not exceed the maximum legal contributions.
- That the political contribution is not tax deductible.

Also, list an address on the page where checks can be mailed and the name of the organization that the contribution should be made out to.

Potential donors won't dig around to find a way to give money, so make it easy for them. Donate links or buttons should be displayed clearly throughout your site.

"Don't treat your online donors
like an ATM machine."

One donation page is never enough

With a single online donation page, you miss the opportunities of segmenting supporters and sending them to targeted pages.

By using specific donation landing pages, you can track conversions from different sources. This can improve donation pushes and maximize your contributions from different donor segments.

Segment your audience. Email or offline fundraising campaigns that target specific supporters by issue, interest, or demographic should send those audiences to tailored landing pages.

Segment your appeals by larger and smaller donors. Try making two pages with different donation ranges, one for smaller donors and another for larger donors. Using different donation forms prevents sticker shock for your lower range donors *and* discourages major donors from giving less than they normally would.

Test what donation pitches works better. You can create variants of your donation page to see which one performs better. To test, send half of your list a link to the first page, and the other half a link to the second page.

If possible, use a unique thank-you message for each donation page. Concrete and compelling thank-you messages will resonate with those that support you – and set the path for further donations.

Many online fundraising services allow you to create multiple donation pages.

Where can you find information on large donors?

The most common way to find potential donors is to check donors of other candidates. Your local party may be able to provide you information. You can search the Federal Election Commission website at fec.gov. It's a bit clunky to use, but you can filter your donor searches through multiple fields, allowing you to identify potential prospects by location, employer, and contribution date and amount.

Acting on trigger events

A *trigger event* is something noteworthy that happens during a campaign. It can be a calendar event, a news story, or something else that may be of importance to your supporters.

Trigger events can often attach an emotional link to a fundraising request. They help promote a higher response rate and work better than a generic appeal for funds.

Email and social media gives you an immediate way to capitalize on trigger events. With some planning, you can keep your fundraising momentum going throughout the campaign.

The political calendar already provides a variety of trigger events on which to request donations. They include:

- Election Day
- Early voting start and deadline
- Primaries
- Rallies
- Press events
- Starting/Nearing/Achieving fundraising goals
- Get out the vote

Trigger events also occur throughout the campaign. They are often based on unplanned events, such as:

- News events related to campaign issues
- Opponent's gaffe or mistake
- Opponent's offensive or inaccurate mailing
- Endorsement announcement
- Opponents support for issue or legislation
- Poll results
- Emergency mobilization

The key is to capitalize on events at the right time. Send a donation request immediately after an opponent makes a large gaffe. Don't wait until it's out of the news cycle. It's tough to create messaging on the fly, so why not create some common appeals ahead of time? Have rough drafts ready so that in the event of a potential trigger, you will be ready to capitalize on it quickly.

Online donation tips

- For many donors, their first online contribution may very well be to your campaign. They will expect your campaign to maintain high standards of privacy and security. Your campaign's policies should reflect this.

- Try to make your donation form blend as seamlessly as possible with your website. This can mean embedding the donation form into a page or having the donation page carry over design elements from the campaign website, such as a logo or site header.

- Use clear language on your Donate or Give Now page. Make the call to action without ambiguity.

- Include a donation button on every website page, but don't bury it. Near the top of a page is the most valuable call-to-action location.

- Only ask for the minimum information needed. The more information you require, the more likely the donor will abandon the page.

- Use messaging to reinforce why they are donating. It can be whatever fits the request, such as, 'For every $25 you give, we can reach another hundred voters.'

- Try asking for less money. Setting the bar low may get you more donors and dollars. Try asking for $10 rather than $35 and see how it works. Once you have a small donation, then you can go back to those donors and ask for higher amounts.

- A theme-based appeal (explaining exactly how a donation will be used) is generally more effective than a generic appeal for funds.

- When mailing letters, always mention that online donations are accepted. People who might not take the time to write a check might be willing to make a quick donation online. This also works well in tandem with phone calls, where your phone bank operators mention that donations are accepted through your campaign website.

- Contact donors repeatedly for additional contributions. Many successful campaigns follow the 'rule of three'. This is where contributors are first asked to contribute early to the campaign, once again in the middle, and then finally again near the end.

- **Recurring donations are great.** Getting donors to commit to repeat, automatic donations throughout the campaign can be powerful. *Some third-party processors allow for this option.*

Holding virtual events

Virtual events are live, in-person events that are happening online. They are the digital equivalent of the live events that many people attend on a regular basis.

Live virtual events provide a more personal and intimate atmosphere than a traditional live event. They allow the organizer to have a conversation with their audience, which can be particularly useful in political campaigns.

There are two types of virtual events that candidates will run:

Virtual Fundraiser: Have the candidate use video conferencing software, like Zoom, to hold a closed-door fundraiser. Donors will appreciate the privacy of this meeting place and be able to communicate with each other more freely. You can run multiple events to keep the number of participants low.

Virtual Political Rallies: These are a way for candidates to connect with voters without the high costs of organizing an event. They provide a way to get the candidate's message out to voters without having to spend money on expensive venues, catering, sound technicians, and other logistical needs.

Virtual Town Hall: A live town hall is a public meeting with the intent to have open dialogue between a political candidate and voters. They are generally held at a public venue (such as a school, library, or community center) and can be streamed online.

There are many benefits for politicians who do live town halls. They can reach more people and get feedback from them directly through their questions and answers.

There are many benefits of virtual events over traditional events. They can save time and money. They also offer more flexibility in scheduling and registration.

Virtual events can be streamed through a variety of channels, including YouTube, Facebook Live and Instagram Live. There are services that specialize in organizing and broadcasting virtual events.

Campaign Town Hall Tools and Services are listed in Appendix A.

Virtual Event Tips

- Send notifications and promote your virtual event as you would for a real event. If your event does not have an attendee limit, ask those you invite to invite others.

- Make sure your lighting, audio and visual equipment is working properly before the event. If you have guests, make sure everything is working well on their end, too.

- Prepare visuals ahead of time. Images and screen shots help keep things interesting during the presentation.

- Have a staffer ready as a co-host or moderator to keep things moving along.

- Set an agenda at the start of the event so everyone knows what to expect, when things will happen and when questions can be asked.

- Have a few supporters ready to ask some questions during the Q&A time to help kick off discussion. You can also invite question submission in advance of the event.

- After the event, send follow-up emails to your participants. Thank them for their support and let them know about any upcoming events.

- Get feedback from participants and staff. Find out what worked and what did not so your next virtual event goes even better.

Want to sell campaign swag?

Rather than order branded campaign merchandise in bulk, you can sell directly through online marketplaces that create items on demand. That way you do not need to store inventory and risk having leftovers after the election.

You can sell campaign items at cost or mark up for additional revenue. Online marketplaces are simple to set up. Just create an account, choose the products you want to sell, and upload your logo or artwork. Typical political swag includes bumper stickers, shirts, buttons, mugs, and stickers.

There are many online marketplace services, including cafepress.com, zazzle.com and spreadshop.com. If you have a WordPress website, you can even use a plugin like *WooCommerce* and tie it into an online payment system.

Making that final fundraising push

As Election Day draws near, don't become complacent. Make that final push for campaign contributions.

Make your final fundraising appeals specific. Let donors know that the money is for a *specific goal that is critical to victory.* For example, you could have one final brochure printed and ready to go, but you need money for the postage. Another example might be that you need to hire more phone bank staffers to help get out the vote.

Target supporters who have already donated, as they already have a stake in the campaign. Your message should be frank, but also a bit alarmist. Remind the reader that the campaign has come too far and is too close to victory to lose because of a lack of money at the finish line.

In the end, be sure you thank your supporters and donors, no matter the outcome.

Campaign Email

Despite the growing popularity of social media, email remains a powerful marketing and outreach tool. Email can help your campaign keep supporters interested and active throughout the campaign. Using email effectively can affect both your online and offline success.

In this section, we will examine the email options available, the concept of the sig file and some tips on campaign email communication.

Let's begin with the easy stuff.

Email address forwards

For small campaigns of short duration, it is usually easier to set up email address forwards, which aliases email from your domain name (e.g., jsmith@johnsmith.com or contact@johnsmith.com) to another email account, such as an internet service provider email account or Gmail account.

There are several advantages to email forwards. First, addresses with the proper domain name in them appear more professional. Forwards allow you to use your existing email accounts rather than monitoring new ones. Finally, you can set a forward to multiple email accounts. This can simplify things if you want to have multiple people notified on incoming messages.

Email forwards can also be set up within a domain. For example, you could have volunteer@johnsmith.com forward to contact@johnsmith.com so that messages sent to either account ends up going to the contact @ address. This can make things easier by having fewer email accounts to maintain.

When using email forwards, make sure you change the reply-to address on your account(s) to match your campaign email account. For example, if you have contact@johnsmith.com forwarded to the address smithformayor@yahoo.com, change the reply-to address of that Yahoo email address to contact@johnsmith.com.

Email forwards can be set up through your web host controls.

Email accounts

There are three ways available to access email with most website hosting accounts. They are *POP, IMAP,* or *Webmail.* Here are the basics about how each works.

POP: POP stands for *Post Office Protocol.* When email is sent, the post office (server) receives it, and then your email program (Outlook, Eudora, etc.) goes to the post office and picks up your mail. The mail is then saved on your computer and is deleted from the server. If your mail is critically important, we recommend running regular backups of your emails.

POP works well if:

- You use one computer to access your email.
- You are the only one who needs access to the email account.
- You sometimes work offline and want access to your email without being connected to the internet.
- You want to keep your mail stored on your local computer so you can easily back it up.

IMAP: IMAP stands for *Internet Message Access Protocol.* IMAP works in an "online" type mode where you connect directly to the server for your mail and all the mail remains on the server, instead of being transferred to your computer. You can create folders on the server to store mail, delete mail, etc. All the work is done on the server. With IMAP you can access that mail account from multiple computers. Although your host should back up email account data, consider keeping a local backup.

IMAP works well if:

- You need to access your email regularly from multiple computers.

- You are on a fast and persistent internet connection.

- You regularly clear out old email and can keep the email in your mailbox under the storage size limit for your account. (Never deleting email that is stored in an IMAP account can cause you to hit your account storage limit. This will cause email to bounce back to senders until the limit is changed or old mail messages are deleted).

Webmail: Most web hosts offer a choice of programs to access email through a web browser. Your host may offer Horde, SquirrelMail, Roundcube or other options. With webmail, all the mail stays on the server. You can access it from any computer that has an internet connection and browser. You log in to webmail through your browser and can read and send messages through it.

Webmail works well if:

- You want to be able to access your email online from multiple computers.

- You would rather check your mail in a web browser and not deal with configuring a program on your computer to handle mail via IMAP or POP.

- You regularly clear out old email and can keep the email in your box under the limit for your account.

- You are traveling and want to access email remotely.

Email setup varies from server to server. Check with your web host for any specific email configuration.

Email signature files

Signature files are a terrific way to promote your campaign. A signature file, commonly known as a sig file, is a short block of information text that you can append to campaign email.

Sig files typically contain the following information:

- Your name.
- Your campaign name.
- A means of contacting your campaign.
- A campaign slogan.

Here is a sample email signature:

Bob Smith, Campaign Director
John Smith for TinyTown Mayor
77 West 20 Street, 6th floor
TinyTown, NY 10001
212.555.7646
800.555.8448
johnsmithforoffice.com

Check your email program's help menu and search for signatures. From there you should find instructions on how to set up a signature for your email messages.

Images, such as campaign logos, can also be added to sig files. Keep in mind that many recipients do not download email graphics or appreciate additional files cluttering up their inboxes. We recommend keeping your signature text or HTML-text only.

Email communication tips

- **Beware the digital divide.** Email is a great tool, and it is tempting to just organize with people who are technically savvy with email, texting, and chat.

However, you could lose good volunteers by only focusing on those with electronic communication.

- **Don't use attachments unless necessary.** Many people can't – or won't – open attachments for fear of viruses. Upload files to your website or an online storage service and provide a link in the message for downloading.

- **Always assume that your opposition could read any message you send via email.** Because email is so easy to forward, sometimes information can find its way to the wrong people. Use a phone if you need discretion.

- **Don't use personal email accounts for mass mailings.** Don't send hundreds of messages through local email accounts (or BCC dozens of recipients at a time). This can cause your account to be blocked by your web host for spamming.

If you plan to send campaign newsletters and updates to a large amount of people, use a bulk email marketing vendor. This is described in the next section.

Action Items

Consider how you want your campaign email configured and what accounts should be set up (contact@, donate@, volunteer@, etc.). Do you want email forwards to existing email accounts? Do you want to set up POP, IMAP, or Webmail accounts? Which campaign staff should have access to campaign email accounts? How should access be controlled?

Campaign Email Marketing

Email marketing is a powerful and effective way to communicate and build a relationship with voters. It can be an important conduit for campaign messaging, including updates on legislative activity, policies, events, and the various aspects of running for office.

Unfortunately, many local candidates do not take advantage of this communication tool. Print advertising gets more attention, but the costs of sending email messages are negligible when compared to print.

Building a subscriber list

The most effective way to obtain a quality email list is to build one yourself. Start this as early as possible. Even without a website, you can still gather addresses – with permission. They can come from personal contacts, event signups, or through donation and volunteer forms (with a checkbox for 'add to email list').

If you can, try to match individuals to the campaign issues that are most important to them. The more information you have on your contacts, the more you can personalize your messaging.

With any email signup form, don't ask for too much information. A name, email address, and maybe a zip code is all that is typically required. Adding a checkbox for those who want to help the campaign is also fine. Asking for more information than that will result in fewer signups.

Your privacy policy

When gathering email addresses, integrity is paramount. Create a clear privacy policy and post it on your website. If you do not sell or rent addresses, note that fact on your signup forms. Many people do not sign up for political email because they are afraid that their information will be shared.

Double opt-in your subscribers

Most legitimate email marketers use a 'double opt-in' method for adding email subscribers. When a new subscriber signs up, a confirmation email is sent to verify that they want to be added to the list. The recipient must authenticate themselves by clicking a link in the confirmation message. Once this is done, the subscriber is added, and they will receive future messages sent to the list.

Double opt-in ensures that no one receives emails that they have not agreed to. This method is also referred to as a 'confirmed subscription' or 'closed-loop opt-in'.

> **Beware of paid email address lists.** Many companies offering email lists for purchase are not scrupulous, and many addresses on their lists have been bought or stolen.

When adding collected emails to your own list, do so as soon as you can after signup. For example, if you collect email addresses from an event, add them within a day. That way, the subscribers will get a confirmation email while they still remember what they had signed up for.

Choosing an email messaging system

Though it is never recommended, it is possible to send bulk email through your own email software, such as Microsoft Outlook or Eudora. There are several drawbacks to doing this. For example, if you use personal software to maintain your campaign email list, you must manually add or remove subscribers. This can become cumbersome as your list grows.

> Bulk-sending email via personal email accounts or through personal email software likely runs afoul against your ISP and your web host's terms of use.

A range of *email messaging services* exist – from free, simple, and unsophisticated systems to more costly, complex systems that are customizable and allow for sophisticated user tracking and segmenting.

For smaller campaigns, free or low-cost email marketing solutions might be enough. For managing multiple newsletters or for user segmenting and targeting, a paid or higher end option is necessary.

Paid email marketing vendors

If you plan to send messages to many email addresses, you will need a *paid email marketing vendor*. These companies have relationships with internet service providers that help ensure that messages get through to recipients.

Email marketing vendors offer advanced tools and functionality, including:

- **Mail merge:** You can automatically insert the member's name, email address, or other information into the text of the message.

- **Automatic subscription and removal of recipient email addresses.**

- **Automatic error processing:** Bad email addresses are automatically flagged in your database and can be easily removed.

- **Trackable URLs:** You can track how many people click on the links in your emails. This feature can be useful in determining the effectiveness of your messages.

- **Segmentation of users** based on activity.

A few of the more popular and affordable email vendors include:

- AWeber.com

- MailChimp.com

- VerticalResponse.com

Political email services exist as well. Some are bundled as part of larger fundraising system or within a CRM.

Most vendors allow you to upload addresses that you have gathered offline. If you import additional user information, you can send targeted broadcasts to users. This user information may include location, issue interest, or whether the recipient is a known donor. Segmenting users can be highly effective, but it takes planning to put it in place. Email segmentation is discussed in more detail below.

> **Tech Tip:** Data services exist that can append additional information to data you already have. For example, you may have an address list, but do not have email or phone information. You can fill in your information gaps though these services.

Email marketing services each provide different features and options. If you can get a trial period, take advantage of the time to test the system. It can be painful to switch vendors in the middle of a campaign.

See Appendix A for a list of email marketing and data append services.

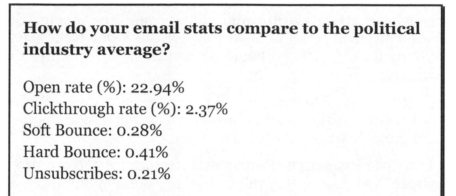

How do your email stats compare to the political industry average?

Open rate (%): 22.94%
Clickthrough rate (%): 2.37%
Soft Bounce: 0.28%
Hard Bounce: 0.41%
Unsubscribes: 0.21%

Source:
https://mailchimp.com/resources/research/email-marketing-benchmarks/

Autoresponders provide multiple touch points

Autoresponders are a great tool for email marketing. They are a series of sequential, follow-up messages that are automatically sent to subscribers. Most autoresponder sequences are seven or so messages – based on the old seven-message marketing rule.

The length of your campaign will influence how many autoresponder messages you'll want to set up. Since you don't know when someone will sign up to your email list, don't make your messages time sensitive. As your campaign ends, you should suspend your autoresponder messages so subscribers don't get automatic emails after the election.

For a political campaign, consider the following autoresponder sequence:

1) Introduction: Brief thank-you for joining the list, along with some basic information about the campaign. This should be sent immediately after the user is added to the list.

2) About the Candidate: Short message about the candidate, giving a bit of history and reasons why he or she is running for office. This should be sent a day or two after the first message.

3) Position Statement: Provide a rundown of the candidate's positions and philosophy. This email and the next three should be spread a few days apart.

4) Online Presence: Promote the features of the campaign website and invite the subscriber to follow the candidate through the site, Facebook, Twitter, or other online avenues.

5) Position Statements: Take one or two of the most important issues and discuss the candidate's position. Spell out the benefit of supporting the candidate. Suggest the recipient get involved with the campaign if they agree and want to help.

6) Wrap-up and Reminders: Highlight the main points of your first two messages to reacquaint yourself with the subscriber. This is important for people who missed earlier messages.

Map out your email narrative ahead of time. Each message should stand-alone, while forming part of a larger theme. Notice that none of the messages are designated solely as volunteer donation solicitations. The focus of these messages is to build awareness and interest so when you send additional requests, they will be better received.

Email broadcast messages

A *broadcast message* is any email sent to your list that is not an autoresponder message. They can be news alerts, event updates or exclusive messages sent to your subscribers.

How often is 'too much' when it comes to sending out messages? The frequency of your messages may become annoying to some, but it's important to keep in close contact, especially as the campaign season heats up and you approach Election Day.

The best way to keep your subscribers engaged is to keep your communications interesting and varied.

Here are some sample email broadcast topics:

Recent campaign events: Keep your supporters up to date. Don't forget to include (or link to) photos, press releases, and other material related to the event.

Information about upcoming events: Provide a list of upcoming events but keep the list short. Use future events as subject matter for additional broadcasts.

Promotional news: Mention where that new, extra-large billboard ad is posted or when the candidate's latest interview will be aired on television. Let your readers know just how much your campaign is growing.

New additions to your website: From news updates to photos from the latest campaign event, don't forget to mention them.

Endorsements: Announce new and current endorsements from prominent individuals and organizations. Add a blurb or two as to why they are supporting your campaign.

Position statement: Use the opportunity to state your position on an existing or new issue.

Requests for volunteer and financial support: Try to tie in your donation request to a specific event or need. Alternate 'fundraising-only' pushes with more informational messages.

Answer common questions: You have probably answered emails from people asking questions about you and your campaign. Use those questions and answers as the subject of your message.

Video posts: Do not try to embed video in your email. Take a screen capture of your video playing, embed that image into your email, and then link to the video itself.

For any autoresponder sequence or broadcast, always assume that your opponent is a recipient. Never send critical or sensitive information to unverified people.

> **Pro Tip:** For ideas on style and format, subscribe to other political campaigns and organization newsletters. Get a feel for how often they ask for support and how they do it. To be on the safe side, sign up with a 'dummy' email account.

Calls to action

In any broadcast, limit your request to a single, clear call to action. Asking for too many things will dilute the request. Typical calls to action include asking people to donate, volunteer, watch a video, read a news article, follow on social media, or even requesting that the recipient forward the message to friends.

Successful emails tend to stick to one topic per message. If you have a few big things to talk about, it's better to send multiple messages then to cram everything into a single message.

Try to weave into every message a reason why the reader should donate or otherwise support your campaign.

People will donate time and money after they have established some level of affinity with a candidate or cause. Turning your newsletter into a broken record of 'send money and volunteer your time' will become tiresome. Specific requests for time and money during a campaign are fine, but if that's all you do, then don't expect much success (or to keep many subscribers).

For contribution requests, it should be made clear where the money is going. This may include specific television or radio ads or a final mailing before Election Day.

Common 'excuses' for donation requests include:

- New polling data (positive or negative).

- A real or perceived slight against the candidate by an opponent.

- Something said or done by an opponent against someone else.

- To promote a new ad campaign.

- To fund a mailing.

- To close a polling or funding gap.

- Final run-up to Election Day.

Build a case for the reader that they should donate *because of what is happening*. This introduces an immediacy effect that spurs action.

Email subject lines

Subject lines are the first thing a reader sees, so they need to be good. You have just a few short words to provide a compelling reason for someone to open the message. Trying to be too 'cute' with the subject line may get your message ignored or, worse, flagged by spam software. Users may delete a subject line that looks too much like spam (e.g., Important Information – Open Now!). Sometimes the best subject lines are the simplest, such as 'John Smith for Mayor – Second Debate Information'.

The optimal length of an email subject line is about seven words or 41 characters.

Use a consistent 'From' name that identifies you as the sender of the message. Most politicians use their campaign name. This helps identify your messages, making it more likely that they recipients will open them. This also gives the reader an easy keyword to add to their spam filter's allow list, ensuring that future messages arrive in their inbox.

> **Tip:** Track the 'open' rates of your messages. That measurement indicates the effectiveness of your subject lines. 'Click' rates indicates the effectiveness of the message itself.

Make it easy to unsubscribe

A sad fact is that some people may want to eventually unsubscribe from your email list. Maybe they are already convinced to vote for you, or maybe they've gone for the other candidate. Whatever the reason, you'll want to make it easy for someone to unsubscribe. If you don't, then people could mark your emails as spam. This can affect the overall deliverability of your future messages.

Paid email services append an automatic disclaimer and unsubscribe links to outgoing messages.

Personalizing your messages

Professional email marketing services do more than just serve email lists. They can also manage specific data about your subscribers. This can include name, email, address, interests, and more. This can be information subscribers provide or it can be information you add about them yourself. When this data is used properly, you can do some interesting things with your messages.

Adding a user's name into a message is the most common form of personalization. To do this, the email system requires that you use placeholder copy such as '{!name}'. When the message is sent, the bracketed information is replaced with the person's name. If you do this with other information, you can further personalize messages and build a greater connection with the recipient.

Personalizing by issue is tougher, especially if the issue not a single word or phrase that can be easily replaced in an email template. That's where *list segmentation* comes in. For example, if you want to send a message about the local traffic issue, you can segment users based on zip code or issues they have listed as important. Targeted messages tend to result in a higher email opening and response rate.

Email list segmentation

No two email subscribers are identical, so why would you treat them all the same? A good *email list segmentation* strategy can lead to better results. It can provide higher open rates and increased conversions.

When using list segmentation, the first step is determining what criteria or factors your segment(s) will be based on. Professional marketers often base their criteria on personal interests, behavior, and demographics. The more data you have on your subscribers, the more personalization you can achieve.

Let's take a closer look at these areas and how they might apply to your campaign.

Segment by Lists

You may want to create separate email lists for specific issues. If you do this, you can let subscribers opt into specific lists when they sign up for updates.

The process for creating and maintaining multiple lists varies between email vendors. Generally, the process involves creating the lists. Then you can create a signup form with checkboxes for each topic/list.

> This strategy isn't advised unless you plan to have many subscribers. It can be difficult maintaining different lists and creating specific content for each.

Segment by Behavior

You can base segmentation on subscriber behavior. You can use open rates, click-through rates, and bounce rate information to measure key indicators such as engagement, responsiveness, and loyalty among your subscribers.

For example, for subscribers that responded to an initial donation email, you can send a follow-up email asking them for a second donation or to become more involved in the campaign in some way.

Segmentation by Demographic

You can create more segmentation options by applying demographic information to your subscriber list. You can segment by age, gender, profession, income, and lifestyle criteria. Segmenting your list is easier when you ask for information when subscribers sign up. You can also combine subscriber information with other data sources.

Some vendors can help you aggregate your existing list with outside data sources.

See Appendix A for email and data resources.

Political email and spam

The CAN-SPAM Act, signed into law in December 2003, established the first national standards for sending commercial email. 'Political spam' often includes email sent from, or on behalf of, a candidate for public office, or in support of a political issue or initiative. These messages do not fall under the legal requirements of commercial email spam under CAN-SPAM.

So, does this mean that you can rent a list of voter email addresses and send messages to them?

Well, you can. As a political candidate, the law and the First Amendment may well protect you when your campaign sends unsolicited political email. But that does not mean you can ignore all legal issues. For example, campaigns that accept federal funds may be required to follow disclosure requirements. In addition, you can be held liable for spreading false or misleading information via email – if that is your purpose.

Spam is generally associated with scams and offensive products. Unsolicited political spam often as unwelcomed to the average voter.

In the end, ISPs are the final arbitrators as to what messages reach inboxes. If they think your messages are spam, there is a chance many of your emails never reach the recipient.

Tracking email success

Web analytics are not limited to web pages and social media. Most email marketing vendors also provide analytic tools. Knowing how your subscribers are interacting with your emails will help you refine and improve your messaging.

These are your most important questions:

Which messages are being opened? How many emails are being read? Are the subject lines effective? Is material at the top of the message interesting enough that a person viewing the message in preview mode would open the message to read it?

Which links are being clicked? Even if the messages are opened, are readers reacting by clicking through to your site, video, or donation page?

How well are your messages converting? Are those clicks converting? What messages are performing best? Are people taking some sort of action?

Which pages of your site are people visiting? Once visitors are on your site, do they leave immediately or stick around? Where do they go? What can you do to keep them from leaving?

By appending your email links, as described in the *Measuring Success* section above, you can track email visitor traffic and activity within your website analytics.

Online Political Advertising

Having your website indexed in the search engines can help attract visitors and traffic. To further reach out and engage your audience, you will want to invest in paid online advertising.

The SMART mnemonic is an approach for creating efficient and successful marketing campaigns. The first-known use of SMART appeared in the November 1981 issue of *Management Review* by George T. Doran.

SMART can act as an approach to plan goals for advertising achievement. For online political advertising, SMART can be defined as:

- *Specific* – Have a specific target for each advertising campaign. This can be voter exposure, issue awareness, fundraising appeals, and so on.

- *Measurable* – Set in place some indicator of progress. This could be the number of people reached or amount of money raised.

- *Assignable* – Who will manage the ad campaigns? It may be one person or several that have experience with a platform. Who is responsible for creating and approving the ads?

- *Realistic* – What results can realistically be achieved, provided you have the available resources. Your second round of fundraising appeals can be larger if money from the first round of fundraising is applied to an ad campaign.

- *Time-related* – Each ad campaign should have a scheduled beginning and ending. For example, a GOTV drive should be near Election Day. Donation appeals generally stop at the end of the campaign.

While business and political online advertising overlap in many ways, the rules are continually changing. More disclosure transparency is required by political advertisers than business advertisers. 'Paid for' disclaimers and sponsor verification are needed by candidate and political issue advertisers. Some online platforms and apps have entirely banned political advertising because of the difficulty in monitoring content.

How much will it cost?

Before we delve into your promotional options, you are probably wondering how much money you should plan to dedicate to online advertising. Like many other aspects to online campaigning, the answer is, 'it depends'. Your budget will depend on what you are running for, the size of your overall campaign and even your location.

You may want to experiment early on to get an idea of how much it costs to reach your target audience.

This can serve a dual purpose. Try starting some online advertising early in the campaign to build awareness. Perhaps you will want to dedicate a small amount of money attracting followers to your campaign Facebook page. Later, you can follow up with some broader Facebook advertising for a campaign event. Early Pay Per Click advertising tests can help you determine what messaging performs best.

Toward the end of your campaign, you can increase your online advertising for early voting and a final get out the vote drive. By that time, you should have a feel for how much money you should be spending.

Again, your online advertising needs will depend on your unique circumstances.

Setting an early outline of your online advertising strategy will help you set goals and make budget decisions as the campaign progresses. Be prepared to change your plans and, if necessary, take on an entirely new direction.

What registered voters should you concentrate on contacting beyond a candidate's party voters?

This depends on your area. Independents and No Party Preference voters are generally split down the middle as far as party preference. If you can segment and reach out to those voters by a specific topic that they care about, you are more likely to succeed with your messaging.

Online advertising has become much more aggressive.

Social media advertising

Social media advertising is a popular tool for political campaigns. This form of advertising can be extremely cost effective and allows for a targeted audience. With the right strategy, social media advertisements can help you reach potential voters who may not have been reached otherwise.

Fortunately, social media advertising is relatively inexpensive. For a fraction of the cost of a television ad, you can run a decent amount of online advertising across multiple platforms.

Advertising platforms change often. Because of this, we will focus on the major ad types rather than the mechanics of setting up specific advertising campaigns.

How and if you use these online advertising options is entirely up to you.

Facebook advertising

https://www.facebook.com/business/products/ads

Getting people to like your campaign on Facebook is just the first step. Don't assume that just because someone simply 'Likes' your page, that they will actively follow your updates. In fact, it is likely that a typical follower will see little of your Page activity.

Facebook determines what posts a user sees in his or her news feed. In theory, the more a user 'engages' a Page, the more likely they will see current updates from that Page.

If you are posting and your natural (or organic) reach is not doing enough for you, paid promotion is another option. Facebook offers a wide variety of ad options that are useful for political campaigns. One of the advantages of advertising on Facebook is the way advertisers can *segment and target ads based on user's interests and demographics, such as location, gender, and age.*

Advertisers running ads about social issues, elections or politics require disclosure that identifies who paid for the ad. This can take some time, so it is best to start this process well before you plan to run any advertising.

> Instagram, which is owned by Facebook, is tied directly into Facebook's advertising offerings.

Advertising Costs

Facebook advertising can be inexpensive. You can promote a post to your followers for a few dollars. You can reach the population of an entire state for a few thousand dollars. The pricing depends mostly on how many people you intend to reach and how long you run your ads.

Advertising Options

There are many advertising opportunities on Facebook and its properties. They tend to change often. The following are goals for Facebook advertising:

Page Post Engagement: This allows you to 'boost' a post to reach more followers than it would organically, or to expose the post to a particular audience. This can get more people seeing, liking, commenting on, and sharing your Page content.

Page Likes: This type of ad is designed to promote your Page and get more people to like your Facebook Page. When someone likes your Page, your posts may appear in their News Feed. You can choose which section of your Page you want people to go to when they click. For example, if you have a donation tab, you can send them directly to that section of your Page.

Clicks to Website: This ad allows you to send people directly to your website from Facebook. When your ad is clicked, visitors can be sent to your home page, donation landing page, volunteer page, or any page you choose. Once you choose an audience, you can set a daily or lifetime budget and then schedule how long you want the ad to run.

Event Responses: With this ad, you create an event that others can add to their own Facebook calendars. Followers get reminders for your event, fundraiser, or appearance. You can keep track of how many people responded to the invite.

Video Views: Videos that are posted directly through Facebook tend to have a higher organic reach. You can engage new audiences more deeply with video than other types of ads.

Conversion Tracking: This feature tracks actions on your website after someone sees or clicks your Facebook ad. You can track newsletter signups, donations, or purchases. Conversions are tracked using a Facebook pixel (special HTML code) on your website. You can view conversion results in your Facebook reports.

For information on setting up and configuring Facebook tracking pixels, visit

https://www.facebook.com/business/help/742478679120153.

With online advertising, it's a good idea to set up conversion tracking. Different advertising systems will provide you with specific tracking code to add to your website pages.

Ad Types and Placement

Facebook offers several different ad types. They include:

- Photo – Within news feeds.

- Video – Before, during or after video content.

- Stories - Customizable, edge-to-edge experience that lets you immerse people in your content.

- Carousel - Show multiple images or videos in a single ad.

- Slideshow - Lightweight video ad for different connection speeds.

Facebook Ads appear differently depending on where your ads are displayed. Ads can be set to appear in the Mobile News Feed, Desktop News Feed, Right Column, on Instagram, and on the Audience Network (third-party mobile apps and mobile websites).

Audience Options

Besides demographic, location, and gender, there are other ways to target specific audiences.

You can target ads to people living in a specific country, state, city, or even zip code.

Connections: This is your first level of connection. These are people who like your Page or your app. When advertising on Facebook, you can also reach the friends of those connections.

Custom Audiences help you target specific people on Facebook based on specific criteria. You can create a Custom Audience based on your contact list, people who have previously visited your website, or people who have behaviors or interests similar to your target audience. If you have more than 1,000 email addresses, you can build a targetable custom audience from it.

Lookalike Audiences let you find an audience who are similar to specific people, such as your best supporters. Use insights and reports from your Facebook marketing to find others who will be receptive to your message.

> **Tip: Create different ad sets for each unique audience.** You can create different ads and deliver them to completely unique audiences. Or you can deliver the same ad to two different audiences and see how they perform. Measuring split testing results can result in better targeting.

For more information on Facebook advertising:

https://www.facebook.com/business/ads

https://www.facebook.com/business/ads/ad-formats

For information on Facebook verification:
https://www.facebook.com/business/help/208949576550051

Twitter advertising

https://ads.twitter.com/

In 2019, Twitter stopped allowing political ads in its platform. This includes issue advertising which Twitter characterizes as ads that "advocate for or against legislative issues of national importance."

The prohibition includes ads that discuss elections, candidates, parties, and other overtly political content. Ads that refer to general causes and are placed by organizations are allowed, but with restrictions. Those restrictions include targeting specific audiences and the mention of specific legislation.

Although you cannot advertise on the Twitter platform, you can still track the effectiveness of your own tweets.

Tweet Analytics

https://analytics.twitter.com

Checking your account analytics can help you optimize your performance on Twitter. The dashboard provides a lot of information, including the ability to:

- Follow performance on a month-by-month basis.

- Track organic and promoted tweet engagements.

- See detailed metrics for specific tweets.

With *Conversion Tracking*, you can measure what happens after users see your posts on Twitter. If people click on a link, retweet, like, or simply see the Tweet and then go to your website, you'll know where they came from. You can see what actions they take on your site, even across devices. To do this, you will need to tag your website pages with tracking code.

Find conversion tracking information at:

https://developer.twitter.com/en/docs/twitter-ads-api/measurement/overview/conversion-tracking

Pay Per Click advertising

Pay per click advertising is one of the easiest ways to target users and deliver traffic via search engines. They are the ads that appear with the natural search results. The way pay-per-click (PPC) works is that you pay each time someone clicks an ad through to your website.

For example, if you buy the keyword phrase 'TinyTown Mayor', your ad will display on the results page when somebody searches for 'TinyTown Mayor.' You are charged when someone clicks on your ad.

Paid placement campaigns can deliver very cost-effective and targeted traffic. However, you will need to budget for this expense.

Google Ads

https://ads.google.com

The Google search engine controls more than half of the web searches on any given day. The Google Ads program displays paid listings that appear above its regular search results.

Besides the Google search engine, advertisers can also appear on other content and affiliate sites.

Google has restrictions on political advertising for US candidates for elected federal or state office, political parties, and state-level ballot measures.

Under these restrictions, only the following criteria may be used to target election ads:

- Geographic location (except radius around a location)

- Age, gender

- Contextual targeting options such as: ad placements, topics, keywords against sites, apps, pages, and videos

Other types of targeting are not allowed for use in election ads. This includes Audience Targeting products, Remarketing, Customer Match, Geographic Radius Targeting, and Third-Party Audiences, such as uploaded lists.

For Google, political content includes ads for political organizations, political parties, political issue advocacy or fundraising, and individual candidates and politicians.

In additions, there are also further restrictions for state and local election ads in some U.S. states.

Verification and disclosure are required to identify who paid for the ad. For most ad formats, Google will automatically generate a "Paid for by" disclosure, using the information provided during the verification process.

This verification process can take time, so you will want to start the process as early as possible.

Political Ad guidelines can be found at:

https://support.google.com/adspolicy/answer/6014595

The Help Center can be found at:

https://support.google.com/google-ads/#topic=7456157

Apply for verification for political ads:
https://support.google.com/adspolicy/answer/9002729

Google AdWord tips

- Give yourself plenty of time for disclosure verification. Don't wait until you are ready to run ads to begin the process.

- Regularly review your keyword search term report. See what users were searching for when your ads were triggered.

- To see the actual searches that trigger your ads, go to your keywords section and then "search terms". If search terms show up in the report that you don't want to advertise on, add them to a *negative keyword list*. For example, if you are running for the Town Board of Tinytown, you might not want your ad to appear on searches for 'Tinytown school elections'. Consider adding the word 'school' as a negative term. *Check the search terms section often to help reduce irrelevant clicks.*

- For accurate ad comparisons when testing multiple ads, turn off 'Automatically optimize ad serving for my ads' in the settings.

- The popularity of your ad will give you an advantage in positioning. Your ad can even rise above someone paying more for a specific keyword. Conversely, if your ad is not successful, it may drop in position, even though your cost per click remains the same.

- *Responsive search ads* let you create an ad that adapts to show more text—and more relevant messages. You can enter multiple headlines and descriptions, and over time, Google Ads will automatically test different combinations and learn which combinations perform best.

- If you set the daily budget limit lower than Google recommends, your ads may not show for all relevant searches.

Google has several editorial guidelines, including:

- No repeated and unnecessary punctuation or symbols.
- Your title may not contain an exclamation point.
- Your ad text may only contain one exclamation point.

These tips can help your ad campaign generate higher click-through rates and lower your cost per click.

- Make sure that your website is ready for traffic.
- Target only specific geographic areas where you want your ads to appear.
- Include keywords in the headline and the description of the ad. For political websites, use the candidate's name in the headline. Include the municipality and elected position in the description, if possible.
- Remove common words from your ads, such as 'a, an, in, on, it, of, etc.'
- Use negative terms to keep your ad from showing up for irrelevant searches. For example, if you are running for school board, you may want to add negative terms such as 'supplies', 'bus' and other unrelated words.
- Include ad extensions to increase your click through rate, improve your ad quality score, and make your ads stand out.
- Test several ads simultaneously. Over time, find out which ads produce the higher click-through rates. Then continue to track and modify your ads. Sometimes reversing a word or two will give you a higher click rate.

- Set up ad campaigns to take advantage of the latest news and developments if they will trigger online searches.

Include the following in your targeted keywords:
- Alternative spellings of your name.
- The name of the race (i.e., Mayor of TinyTown, TinyTown Mayor Election).
- Key issues in the race (i.e., traffic in TinyTown, TinyTown traffic).
- Your opponent's name.
- Your location, including town, county, etc.
- Phrases related to specific issues.

Send visitors to the proper page on your site. If an ad is about a specific issue, send visitors to the specific page addressing the topic. If you don't have one, create landing pages specifically for your PPC audiences.

What does a PPC ad cost? Again, the answer is, 'it depends'. You can easily look to spend at least a dollar a click. Many factors go into an average click cost, including advertiser competition, the specific search keyword, and even the landing page.

Using Google Ads as an online focus group

Google Ads is a great source of data about your voters and their sentiment. It's a tool that can simultaneously reach out to voters while providing research insights about them. And the cost – well, it's a lot less than paying for a live focus group.

Online advertising's strength lies in its agility. Political ad campaigns can be created, modified, and deleted rapidly. Campaign messaging can be modified on the fly by using actual performance data. If something works very well, push it. If something is not getting much action, kill it.

Here is an example of effectively using PPC ad data: After the passage of the Affordable Care Act in 2010, <u>the RNC ran a $50 PPC test</u> to measure the effectiveness of various ad messages. Of all the variations tested, 'Fire Nancy Pelosi' received far and away the most clicks. This phrase became the cornerstone of a massive fundraising campaign that brought the RNC $1.6 million in donations in just three days.

Instead of spending a large amount of money and gambling on a new message, run a Google Ads campaign. Use the response rate to gauge which ad message is the most effective. From there, it's a matter of making multiple versions of your most successful ads. Tweak the headline and copy and let the most successful versions dominate.

> **Tip:** Run a small Google Ads campaign to test new advertising messaging.

The tricky part comes in knowing what a statistically relevant number of ad impressions and clicks make for a good test. Very targeted or small campaigns may have few impressions, and even fewer clicks. This makes it difficult to tell statistically which ads are more effective. A rough number is to use at least 200 clicks before determining if one ad is performing better than another. If one ad is greatly outperforming, you may be able to weed out 'losers' quickly. It's all about keeping an eye on the numbers.

The more time given for testing and the more impressions your ad receives, the more accurate your results will be. With enough time, you will be able to pick the winning ads with the highest click through rate (CTR).

Besides keyword and title optimization, you can also test ad copy. Optimizing pay-per-click advertising is an entire business niche in and of itself. Many consultants specialize in this line of work.

Most campaigns fail to capitalize on testing and split testing. They end up spending more money than they need to or fail to find the ads that get voters to click most.

PPC also allows you to take advantage of current events. If people are searching for a breaking news event, paid advertising can help get your message out fast.

Pay per click tracking

Carefully monitor your PPC campaigns. It's very easy to spend more than you want on terms that aren't helping you. Properly setting up your account goes a long way toward targeting the right terms and demographic.

Use "negative keywords" in your ad groups. This helps keep your spend rate down and prevents your ads from appearing when you do not want or need them.

Google Ads provides detailed reporting and the ability to track click-throughs and conversions. By tracking conversions on actions (such as donations or volunteer form submissions), you can tell what ads are performing best.

By using Google Analytics and Google Ads under the same Google account, you can pull your advertising data into your analytics, including costs and keyword information.

> **PPC Facts**
> ~ Mobile devices account for 53% of paid-search clicks.
> ~ The top 3 paid advertising spots get 46% of the clicks on the page.
> ~ 36% of searches on Google are associated with location.
> ~ The first Google ad goes back to the year 2000. It was for live mail-order lobsters.
> *Source:* https://www.powertraffick.com/ppc-trends-and-statistics

What about Bing Ads?

ads.microsoft.com/

This Microsoft PPC service delivers paid search results for both the Bing and Yahoo! search engines and their partner sites. As of 2019, *Bing Ads disallows advertising for election related content, political parties, candidates, and ballot measures.*

Google Display Ads

Display ads (banner ads) are another way to visually expand your exposure to voters.

Unlike traditional PPC advertising, display advertising is not based on user searches. Rather, the graphic (image) ads appear within the web content that a user is browsing. Display ads are distributed through the *Google Display Network*, which includes a vast network of websites, videos, and apps.

Ads can appear where a user is reading news articles, checking email, or watching online videos.

Display ads give you control over your branding. This differs from traditional Google Search Ads, where the ads are text-based, containing headlines and descriptions.

Again, Google restricts targeting for political election ads. Only the following criteria may be used to target election ads:

- Geographic location (except radius around a location)

- Age, gender

- Contextual targeting options such as: ad placements, topics, keywords against sites, apps, pages, and videos

Disclaimer information is also required for political ads.

These rules apply to political organizations, political parties, political issue advocacy or fundraising, and individual candidates and politicians.

There are two types of Google display ads: *Uploaded ads* are images created by the advertiser. Best practices for uploaded display ads include having a border around the ad, a head shot to make the image more visually attracting and a political disclaimer.

Sample display ad.

Responsive ads are created by uploading your logo, some visual assets (images and videos) and display text. From there, Google Ads will test different combinations of visuals and copy to determine which versions of your ad perform best. Responsive display ads adjust themselves to meet the requirements of specific web pages.

Ads can link to your campaign website or to a landing page. For example, if you are running ads about an issue or ballot measure, have the landing page be about that issue, rather than to your website's home page.

Display ads are great for building awareness. They can be bought on both a cost per impression and through pay per click search models. Voters may not be actively searching for you or your campaign but running display ads across broad search terms allows you to introduce your campaign to a new audience.

Don't forget about verification

Just like with traditional PPC, any individual or organization that purchases an election ad on Google or YouTube must be verified. This verification process takes time, so start the process as soon as you can.

As a final note, changes you make in the Display Network can take 12-24 hours to apply and may not show right away. Keep this in mind while creating a new ad campaign or making changes to an existing one.

And remember to add an *end date* to all your ad campaigns, so they won't appear after Election Day.

For more information, visit:

https://ads.google.com/home/campaigns/display-ads/

Apply for verification for political ads:

https://support.google.com/adspolicy/answer/9002729

YouTube advertising

https://www.youtube.com/ads/

YouTube provides a wide variety of video ad options. It can be an effective marketing channel due to its ability to target specific audiences by interests and keywords, and its ability to measure results through metrics such as views, click through rates, and amount of video time watched.

YouTube advertising can be placed both within videos (in-stream), on the YouTube website itself, and across the Display Network.

> **TrueView in-stream ads** run on videos served on YouTube or on a collection of sites and apps in the Google Display Network (GDN). These ads may also run on YouTube videos that are embedded on other sites or apps.

Skippable in-stream video ads play before, during, or after other videos. After 5 seconds, the viewer has an option to skip the ad. You pay when a person watches the first 30 seconds or interacts with your video, whichever comes first.

Non-skippable in-stream must be watched before a video can be viewed. This ad format designed to allow you to reach customers with your entire message. You pay based on impressions. Non-skippable ads use target CPM (cost-per-thousand impressions) bidding.

Bumper ads are non-skippable, 6-second-long ads that show as a pre, mid or post-roll. They are good for reach and awareness campaigns.

Overlay image or text ads that can appear on the lower 20% portion of a video

Discovery ads appear along with organic search results. They consist of a thumbnail image from your video with text. While the exact size and appearance of the ad may vary depending on where it appears, discovery ads always invite people to click to watch the video. If clicked, the ad sends people to the video page or YouTube channel. You are charged only when viewers choose to watch your ad by clicking the thumbnail.

YouTube Advertising Tips

As with other Google ad offerings, political advertisers are required to be verified by Google.

Separate In-Search and In-Display formats into their own campaigns. Both formats perform differently, and it is easier to evaluate performance and adjust bidding if they are separated.

Set your budgets low to start. Unlike paid searches, where you may not hit your daily budget, YouTube campaigns will generally hit their cost target.

Target your advertising as best you can with demographics (like targeting only voting age viewers) and interests.

For more information about TrueView advertising, ad specs, and formats, visit:

https://support.google.com/youtube/answer/2467968

Retargeting

Retargeting, also known as *remarketing*, is a popular online advertising technique. It displays advertisements to people who have shown an interest in your campaign.

Retargeting tags online users when they visit a web page or open an email. The advertiser is then able to show display ads to that user elsewhere on the web through *ad exchanges*.

Retailers have had success with this advertising method. You have likely been retargeted if you visited an airline website and then later saw ads for flights on other websites.

> Retargeting can help increase awareness and engage interested voters through Election Day.

So, how does retargeting work - and how can it help your campaign?

When a user goes to your website, a tracking pixel is set in the user's browser. For a predetermined period afterward, the user will see display banners about your campaign on other 'partner' websites as they surf the web. Retargeting keeps your campaign fresh in their minds. It can increase return visits and donation/email signup/volunteer conversions.

Retargeting is different from regular pay-per-click advertising or regular media buys. With retargeting, you can segment and target users that visit specific parts of your site, such as issue, volunteer, or donation pages. Segmented visitors can be shown more specific advertising.

Retargeting success can be measured with both *click-through* and *view-through* conversions.

Click-through conversions are conversions that happen as a direct result of someone clicking a retargeting ad.

View-through conversions are a little different. They are conversions that can be attributed to another channel (such as a direct site visit or through a regular PPC ad), but the person was, at some point, served a retargeting ad.

Like PPC advertising, it is a good idea to split-test ads to see which ones resonate best.

You do not need a large budget to do retargeting marketing. For example, with *retargeting ad networks* like Perfect Audience, you can start a campaign with a low weekly budget. Your ads appear to retargeted visitors across a variety of websites that display those ad networks.

Facebook offers its own retargeting service. You can choose to retarget an audience as an advertising option. After tagging your pages with some code, Facebook retargeting will show your ads to visitors who go to your site and later visit Facebook and its related sites, like Messenger and Instagram. Your ads can be designed to send visitors back to your website or to your Facebook page.

For more information, visit

https://www.facebook.com/business/products/ads

It is possible to target the same audience across multiple platforms. For example, you can set up a Facebook retargeting campaign through a retargeting ad network. If you run a retargeting ad campaign through a network and directly through Facebook, you could end up overlapping your efforts.

Retargeting provides an affordable advertising option that is worth pursuing for brand awareness and reach. It only requires tracking code to be installed in your website. (And a budget, of course.)

> **Warning:** With the ongoing changes in online political advertising, it is possible that retargeting ads may fall under additional restrictions at some point.

Retargeting Tips

Retargeting is its own channel. Get to know how your program will work, how it is measured, and what goals you are trying to achieve.

Ads should be catchy. The ads in retargeting campaigns are typically banners or graphics. You'll want to make them both recognizable and interesting to the viewer. Remember, the audience has already been to your website, so they are likely more familiar with you.

Use the same disclaimers on your retargeting ads that you would on any online advertising channel.

It will take time. You will need some time before you find what works right for you. The larger your audience, the faster you will gain actionable information.

IP Targeting

Are you looking to *reach out* to specific voter households with online advertising? If so, then **IP targeting** might be your solution.

IP targeting delivers advertisements to a *pre-determined audience*. You choose who you want to show your ads to. Unlike other types of online advertising, the user doesn't need to be searching for you to see your ads.

IP targeting works by using technology to match IP addresses to a list of street addresses. Then your digital banner or video ads are displayed only to those targeted addresses.

Your ads appear on all household devices – home computers, tablets, cell phones – any device that someone uses to access the web. By tapping into online advertising networks, your ads show on news sites, email portals and other popular websites.

You can tailor and target messaging to a specific audience for greater impact and response. Because of this, IP-targeted ads tend to have a higher click-through rate than PPC or retargeting campaigns.

To run an IP targeting ad campaign, you will need a target address list. This list can be your supporters, members of your political party or addresses of a pre-determined demographic. You will also need a series of banner ads of assorted sizes for mobile and desktop display.

Popular IP Targeting display ad sizes (in pixels):

300×250 - Medium Rectangle
336×280 – Medium Rectangle
300×600 – Half-Page
728×90 - Leaderboard
320×100 - Mobile Banner
160×600 - Wide Skyscraper
320×50 - Mobile Leaderboard

Finally, you will need a landing page for those that click on the ads. Depending on your ad, this can be your website's home page or an informational page of some type.

IP targeting works well when combined with direct mail. It helps reinforce your messaging and branding. Running an IP targeting campaign before your direct mail drops increases the likelihood that voters will take notice when your mailer hits their mailbox.

> Typical uses for political IP targeting include increasing general exposure and encouraging supporter turnout in GOTV efforts.

IP targeting won't reach everyone. Depending on the quality of your list, you can expect 50-95% of your physical addresses to be matched for targeting. Match rates can vary depending on the quality of the list, recent household IP changes and other factors.

As with other forms of online political advertising, be prepared to submit detailed information about your campaign. You will also need to follow specific rules, such as including 'paid for by' disclaimers on every ad.

> **Need address lists?** You can obtain official voter lists from your local county government. However, those lists may not include certain contact and demographic information that you need to refine your targeting efforts. With data-appending services, you can upload your names and postal addresses, then have email addresses and other attributes added to your list data.

How much does IP targeting cost?

The price varies, but it is based on a cost per thousand impression (CPM) model. For example, if you had a final list of 5,000 households and you wanted to display 30 ads to each in a week, you have a total of 150,000 ad impressions. If the CPM cost is $25, then the price for that ad campaign would be $3,750 – or $.75 per household.

Some online advertising agencies provide IP targeting services, others provide IP targeting exclusively. To set up an effective campaign, you may want to go with a firm that has experience working with political organizations.

See Appendix A for IP targeting and voter data services.

Banner advertising

Banner graphics are commonly used in retargeting campaigns and on other online advertising venues, such as newspaper websites.

Traditional banner ads have click-through rates of less than one-half of one percent. However, branding and messaging is generally the more important purpose.

Some publishers will design a creative ad ('creative') for you, although advertisers usually submit their own creatives.

Online ad options have expanded beyond the typical rectangular image. Display ads include pop-ups, ads that race across your screen and even half-page advertisements.

Standards vary by publisher, but typical website ads include:

- **Leaderboard:** 728 pixels wide by 90 pixels tall
- **Banner:** 468 pixels wide by 60 pixels tall
- **Skyscraper:** 120 pixels wide by 600 pixels tall
- **Medium Rectangle:** 300 pixels wide by 250 pixels tall
- **Half-Page:** 300 pixels wide by 600 pixels tall
- **HTML banner:** This is a banner ad using HTML elements, often including interactive forms, instead of (or in addition to) standard graphical elements.
- **Interstitial:** An advertisement that loads between two content pages.
- **Pop-up ad:** An ad that displays in a new browser window above the current browser window.
- **Pop-under ad:** An ad that displays in a new browser window behind the current browser window.

Most online advertising is bought either on a flat rate or through a Cost Per Thousand (CPM) model. The total price of a CPM advertising campaign is calculated by multiplying the CPM rate by the number of CPM units. For example, 100,000 ad impressions at a $10 CPM costs $1,000.

To calculate the amount paid per impression, divide the CPM by 1,000. For example, a $10 CPM equals $.01 per impression.

Banner advertising tips

- Use simple designs that can be scanned and read in just a few seconds.

- If you are advertising on a website, a reputable publisher should be able to provide advertising statistics, including overall page views and unique website visitors. If they cannot do this for you, beware.

- Frequently rotate and split test your banners. It may help to have two or more banners running at the same time to test which has better performance. This is especially important with retargeting ads.

- Track your advertising activity through analytics to determine the effectiveness of your ads and conversions for email signups, donations, etc.

See Appendix A for online promotional services.

Online Ad Archives

The major social media platforms (Facebook, Google, and Twitter) track political advertisers and make those ads available to the public.

The Facebook Ad Library provides a searchable collection of all current and past social issue, election, and political ads from across the various Facebook entities. Ads are kept in the library for seven years.

Use the library for inspiration in your own advertising. You can spy on opponents to see what audiences they are targeting and what issues they are promoting.

Visit https://www.facebook.com/politicalcontentads

Google also provides transparency in political advertising on Google, YouTube, and partner properties. You can find information about ads featuring current elected federal officeholders and candidates for the US House of Representatives, US Senate, President or Vice President. However, its transparency reports are not as easy to use as Facebook's Library.

Visit
https://transparencyreport.google.com/political-ads/region/US

Twitter's Ads Transparency Center (ATC) allows anyone to view political ads that have been served on Twitter. *Ads for federal or general elections are no longer allowed.* You can download an archive of political and issue ads that ran from May 24, 2018, to November 22, 2019.

Visit https://ads.twitter.com/transparency

Take advantage of these ad transparency tools to learn about your opponent's online advertising strategy. Knowing what they've done in past elections can provide insight into what they might do in the future. Getting a heads up on brand new ads can give you an opportunity to respond early and effectively.

Mobile Campaigning

As mobile computing blurs the line between online and offline, many political campaigns now include mobile strategies to their campaign advertising arsenal.

Text messaging

Text messaging has become a major player in the political arena. It is a low cost, high-reaching marketing tool that can convey a message to thousands of people immediately.

One advantage of text messaging over other communication systems (such as email) is that text has an extremely high delivery rate. Recipients opt-in to receive texts, and *a vast majority of the sent text messages are read.*

The texting process

Personal mobile phone plans often allow unlimited text messages each month. But sending texts to hundreds of recipients may cause you problems with your provider.

Software exists that allows users to send messages from a PC or Mac. There are also websites that allow you to send text messages online. However, these methods are *not* an effective way to build and administer a large list of text subscribers.

Creating a robust mobile messaging program is simple. Once you create an account with a *short message service* (SMS), you can pick a keyword for your campaign. People then opt-in to your messaging list by texting that keyword to a number. (Ex: Text SMITH4GOV to 555432.) Then that person will get your text message alerts through the SMS going forward.

Campaigns use SMS to:

- Quickly update supporters on key issues
- Organize rallies

- Broadcast volunteer opportunities
- Inform supporters about fundraising events
- Notify voters and constituents about legislative happenings
- Get Out the Vote and Election Day reminders

Mobile campaigning really took off in the 2012 US elections. An early study showed that text message reminders increased a new voter's likelihood of voting by 4.2 percentage points. That difference in voter participation can mean the difference between an election victory and loss.

Text messaging and SMS are not just for candidates with deep pockets. Mobile texting services start for as little as $20/month. Some services let you send unlimited messages to a maximum number of subscribers. Others charge by the message. Your campaign size and number of potential subscribers will determine what type of package is best for you. You can usually upgrade your package as your subscribers grow.

Promoting candidate text alerts can be done both online and offline. Most services allow you to create special links or widgets that allow text signups directly through your website. Signup instructions can also be added to your print materials.

By starting early, you can build up a large list of people who can be alerted to new campaign announcements and messages as they happen.

Many SMS services allow for a free trial. Test the service to be sure it is one you will want to stick with. Changing SMS providers during a campaign can be tricky.

As mobile campaigning has become more prevalent, several text messaging services now cater to political campaigns.

See Appendix A for a list of text messaging vendors.

Here are some basic mobile messaging definitions:

- **SMS:** Short Message Service (text only, limited to 160 characters).

- **MMS:** Multimedia Message Service (text and images, gifs, or video).

- **Shortcode:** A 5 or 6-digit number used to send and receive SMS or MMS text messages.

- **Keyword:** Word or phrase sent to your shortcode to subscribe to your text messaging campaign.

- **Long code:** A 10-digit phone number, typically used for one-to-one texting. Limited to one message per second.

Texting has its own rules and etiquette. Here are some tips for making your texts more effective.

Identify yourself. Always identify your organization in any text messages you send, even if you have a dedicated shortcode. This is especially important with shared shortcodes where other organizations send messages from the same number. Text message sender identification is required by law. In the US, sender requirements are enforced by the Telephone Consumer Protection Act (TCPA).

It is illegal to buy or acquire phone numbers and send them text messages without express written consent.

Watch your messaging. Just because someone is a supporter of your campaign does not mean that they want to hear from you constantly. Each SMS should have a clear, simple goal. Most text messages are read within 90 seconds of delivery. If you waste a recipient's time and trust, they will opt-out.

Build out your own SMS list. Sending unsolicited texts can cause your number to be block-listed by phone carriers. Do not rent phone lists.

Use a link shortening service. You have limited space in your SMS messages. A link shortening service will save you characters. Most link shortening services allow you to track click metrics, so you can learn which messages get the best response. *See Appendix A for link shortening services.*

Bury your hyperlinks. Don't place a link at the start or end of your text message. On many iPhones, a link is shown as a preview before it can be clicked through. To avoid this, place your hyperlink somewhere in the middle of your message.

Campaign apps

Mobile phone apps increase the connectivity possibilities with constituents and supporters. Common uses for apps include the transmission of campaign news, videos, photos, user surveys and information about coming events. And, of course, they are used for donation solicitations.

During his successful 2008 US presidential campaign, Barack Obama was the first candidate to use smart phone technology to raise a large amount of money. Obama's campaign app listed his position on issues, enabled supporters to follow news feeds, track events, and make donations.

Apps are making an impact in state elections and ballot initiatives. Some apps can tie into databases to link where undecided voters and supporters live and allow canvassers to update voter data and make reports in real-time. Other apps enable users to sign voter ballot initiatives.

At this point, mobile apps tend to be custom-built and priced out of reach for many smaller campaigns, though several vendors specialize in political mobile app development.

For local campaigns, creating a campaign app is probably not worth the time and effort. It is better to focus on your website, social media, and email outreach.

Some campaigning services, such a voter outreach, incorporate apps into their functionality. This is different than building a custom campaign app to keep supporters up to date.

See Appendix A for phone app vendors.

QR Codes

QR stands for "Quick Response." A QR code is a kind of barcode that stores information as a series of pixels in a square-shaped grid. They are used in marketing and advertising campaigns. QR codes can be easily read by a digital device, such as a mobile phone.

A sample QR code.

When scanned by a mobile device, the QR code allows immediate information access, such as a link to an app, a download or web page. They can also be used for SMS signups.

QR codes have been around since 1994. They had a brief spurt of popularity some years back. After falling to relative obscurity, QR codes gained new life in 2020 when the pandemic increased the need for touch-free delivery, pickup, and payments.

Some campaigns use QR codes on brochures, posters, and yard signs. They are often used to direct a user to a web page. However, they can also be used as links for donation pages or online polls. By using UTM parameters in the links, QR codes can even be used for source tracking.

Are QR codes essential to online campaigning? Not really. But if you are interested in using them, there are free tools that allow you to create QR graphics.

Visit https://www.qr-code-generator.com

Virtual Volunteering

Campaigning online has lots of benefits. For instance, volunteers can work remotely. There are plenty of remote jobs which they can do partly or completely if they have access to the internet through a computer or mobile device.

Online volunteers can provide a variety of tasks, including:

- Phone calls, phone banking and outreach
- Email creation and editing
- Video creation and editing
- Graphic design - print and social media
- Web design and content updates
- Social media updates
- Remote training

Because virtual volunteering is flexible and can be done from almost anywhere, you may find people willing to help online. As with any other volunteer, you'll want to vet them properly.

Volunteers should either have experience or training in the jobs to which they are assigned.

Virtual volunteers need direction and supervision. It's easy to let someone who knows what they are doing to go off and 'do their own thing'. You wouldn't let canvassers go door-to-door without some plan of where they are going and what they are supposed to say.

Give volunteers autonomy as they gain experience, while continuing to provide the training and support they need. Volunteers who work in isolation often do not have the kind of experiences that lead to long-term engagement. It's important to keep in touch with virtual volunteers and encourage them to work with other individuals and groups.

> There will be peaks and plateaus throughout the campaign. Let your workers know regularly about the progress being made, and how their efforts make a difference.

Everything a volunteer does reflects on the organization. It's important to track what online volunteers are doing and to set specific task guidelines.

The role of a *volunteer coordinator* is to organize and manage the volunteers in a campaign. For example, they need to make sure that each volunteer knows their job and how they can best contribute to the campaign. They can create tasks, collaborate, set goals, and measure performance through a CRM.

It takes work to leverage virtual volunteers effectively. There may volunteers with valuable skills, while others may only be able to perform simple tasks. When volunteers are given responsibilities suitable to their abilities, they feel more invested and interested in the organization.

Candidate Training Programs

In recent years, many organizations and schools have put together online training programs to help political candidates and staff learn important campaigning skills.

Many of the courses listed below are non-partisan, and most are free.

American Majority

americanmajorityonline.org

Non-partisan, nonprofit that continually trains, organizes, mobilizes, and equips new grassroots conservative leaders. Offers in person and online training.

Arena

arena.run

Provides training to aspiring campaign staff, with a focus on recruiting and supporting women, people of color, and members of the LGBTQ+ community. Offers *Arena Academies*, a five-day intensive web training program.

Asian Pacific American Institute for Congressional Studies (APAICS)

apaics.org

A national non-partisan, nonprofit organization dedicated to promoting Asian Pacific American participation and representation at all levels of the political process, from community service to elected office.

Blue Institute

theblue.institute

Focusing on the South and Southwest, the Blue Institute works to bring more young people of color to become leaders, strategists, and key staff members of progressive electoral campaigns and organizations.

Collective PAC

collectivepac.org

Their mission is to build Black political power through educating and equipping voters, donors and candidates with trainings, technical assistance, advertising, and fundraising.

Dare to Run

daretorun.org/upcoming-webinars

Offers women candidates the chance to participate in a one-year certificate program in pursuit of a career path in public service.

Democracy for America (DFA)

democracyforamerica.com/site/events/category/online-trainings

Building and empowering a broad coalition of grassroots organizers to elect people of color and white progressives to fight for inclusive populism at all levels of office in all 50 states.

Elevate

ncil.org/elevate

Helps people with disabilities learn how they can run for office to represent their community. Offers a series of webinars that teach core campaigning skills.

Emerge America

emergeamerica.org/candidate-training

Recruits, trains, and provides a powerful network to Democratic women who want to run for office. Offers several boot camps and longer training opportunities.

Emily's List

emilyslist.org/run-to-win/trainings

Helps train Democratic women. The *Ignite Change Fellowship* is an eight-week virtual training initiative designed for community leaders, organizers, and advocates to develop their political skills and confidence.

Federal Election Commission Training

fec.gov/help-candidates-and-committees/trainings

Each year, the FEC hosts two-day regional conferences where Commissioners and staff conduct a variety of technical workshops on the law. Discussion topics include fundraising, reporting and communications.

Higher Heights for America

higherheightsforamerica.org/webinars

National organization providing Black women with a political home dedicated to harnessing their power to expand elected representation, voting participation, and progressive policies.

IGNITE

ignitenational.org/calendar

Hosts online events and trainings to accelerate young women's path to political power.

National Democratic Training Committee

traindemocrats.org

Free, in-depth training for Democrats who want to run, work, or volunteer on campaigns.

National Women's Political Caucus

nwpc.teachable.com/p/nwpc-online-campaign-training

Supports pro-choice women running for elected and appointed office. Fee required for non-members.

Ready to Run

cawp.rutgers.edu/education_training/ready_to_run/overview

A national network of non-partisan programs to encourage women to run for elective office, position themselves for appointive office, work on a campaign, or get involved in public life in other ways.

Re:Power

repower.org/events

Originally *Wellstone Action*. Offers long-term technology skills building, support, and training around digital organizing, engineering, digital security, data and analytics for campaigns and grassroots movements.

Running Start

runningstartonline.org

Nonpartisan nonprofit that trains young women to run for public office. For high school and college-level students.

She Should Run

sheshouldrun.org/explore/road-to-run

A virtual event series that provides women a starting place for considering and exploring a future run for office as well as a baseline knowledge of what goes into campaigning.

Women's Public Leadership Network

training.womenspublicleadership.net

With comprehensive online training and a network of state-based partners, their mission is to educate, organize, and inspire women to seek public office.

The Campaign School at Yale

tcsyale.org

Provides a nonpartisan, issue-neutral training program to increase the number and influence of women in elected and appointed positions. Tuition required for live online session.

Online courses are not the only way to get political training. There are many other opportunities for candidates to get education in-person or through more intensive programs that focus on just one aspect of campaigning.

Election Laws

Although the web is often considered a freewheeling environment, local election laws still apply to online political campaigning. As a candidate, it is essential to know the rules that apply online before you start your digital campaign.

Here are some general legal topics to keep in mind as you start your campaign:

When can you start campaigning?

Some states or municipalities have restrictions on when you can actively start campaigning. Some laws are more restrictive than others – especially for judicial campaigns. Even if you must wait, many candidates prepare ahead of time. They may reserve a domain name and get their website ready in anticipation of the time that they can go 'live' with it.

Website disclaimers

You may need a disclaimer or certain verbiage in your site footer or elsewhere on your site. Generally, this would match the requirements of your printed materials. Online political ads also require disclaimers and owner verification before they can run on an advertising platform.

Restrictions on what can appear on your campaign website

There may be restrictions on the use of state flags or state seals in the design. (We're looking at you, Florida.) They may be additional restrictions as to whether you can appear in uniform in campaign materials. This issue comes up often in law enforcement and sheriff campaigns.

What you can say on your site

Occasionally we have had a candidate change their website header after they discover that they cannot use certain phrases or words. In one case, we had to remove the word 'Elect' from the header because the election laws for the position did not allow for that word to be used at all. Be aware of how your web content, print copy and signage reads so it does not give the impression that the new position you are running for is a position you already hold.

How you can contact voters

With the increase in texting, robocalls and phone banks, there are still rules that political campaigns must follow. In 2020, congress passed the TRACED Act to combat illegal robocalls. It increased potential fines and added additional tools for regulators to combat spam calls and texts.

For example, calls to cell phones are prohibited unless the recipient has explicitly opted-in to receive campaign updates. The message itself must identify the candidate and party for whom call is made. It must also include a contact number and address at the end of the message. Your state may have additional rules and requirements for mobile outreach.

Finance limits

Do not exceed your local campaign contribution limits. Your donation page should be configured to reject donations that exceed your limit. Additional donor information may also be required. This may include, but is not limited to, a donor's occupation, a spouse name, and citizenship requirements.

Invoicing for internet services

If you pay for online services, keep records of your expenses, just as you would for anything else related to your campaign.

Cancel services when you do not need them anymore. Some may have recurring billing, and it's easy to forget about them after Election Day.

Become familiar with your local election laws before you start actively campaigning. Getting caught breaking the rules – even seemingly innocent ones – can be an embarrassing and unnecessary distraction.

Just stick to the letter and the spirit of the law, and you should have no problems at all. *Legally*, at least.

Tying it All Together

Get Out the Vote online strategies

A final Get Out the Vote drive can mean the difference between winning and losing a primary or general election. Your GOTV push should be performed both offline and online to remind supporters that without their vote you cannot win.

As the days count down, increase your online contact through existing communication channels. This may include increasing the frequency of blog posts, email/text messaging and social media updates. Promote the latest news, campaign activities, endorsements, and media coverage. Supporters follow your campaign in many ways, so push updates and reminders across the different channels.

Add voting information to your website. Dedicate a page on your site for information about local voting registration and voting locations. Embedded tools from sites like vote.org, voteamerica.com, and wecanvote.us provide state-specific information for voters.

Consider starting or increasing online advertising. Both Google Ads and Facebook offer targeted advertising options. If you have the budget, run banner ads on local newspaper websites. Target your likely voters through IP targeting. Flood the online market with advertising to appear as if your support has surged.

Traditional newspaper readers tend to skew to an older demographic. News outlets are valuable for campaigns because people who follow local news tend to be more strongly engaged in their communities and vote more often.

Requests for final donations and volunteers should increase as Election Day nears. Specific appeals, such as for a final mailing or campaign ad, tend to do better than generic appeals. Volunteer requests to supporters can be more targeted as well. You may want to ask for poll monitors and Election Day drivers.

Plan out contact points over the last few weeks and days of the campaign. Final reminders should include the date of the Election, absentee voting information, where voting locations exist and when they are open, and contact information for those who need a ride to the polls. Encourage supporters to bring their friends and relatives to vote.

Of course, your GOTV contact is not limited to online efforts. Door-to-door canvassing, texting, and phone banks staffed by enthusiastic volunteers remain a powerful mobilization tactic.

A well-planned, comprehensive GOTV strategy is crucial. It can mean the difference between winning and losing the election.

Planning for the end

Election Day has come and gone. The campaign is over. The advertising has ended. The signs have all come down. But don't forget your online campaign – it will still be out there.

Here are some tips for dealing with your digital presence after Election Day.

Make a final website update

No matter what you do, you should post a final election update to your campaign website. Win or lose, you should acknowledge the results. Thank your friends and supporters for their help – they deserve it.

If you have a domain name that is year-based (electsmith2020.com), you should keep the website up for a few months, or until the end of your hosting period. Your site will still get traffic from those interested in the election outcome. With a date-based name, odds are you won't use that same name/website again. If you have a name that is position or name-based (smithforsupervisor.com or joesmith.com), consider the long-term benefits of keeping the site active versus shutting the site down completely.

You may want to disable certain pages or sections of the website but continue to post news updates. Keep the interest alive until the next campaign.

If you are finished with politics, your website can be redesigned and re-purposed for another use. If you run a business in your name, you can switch the entire site over to a new venture.

Redirect your domain name

Instead of having the domain name point to your campaign website, point it to another website or web page. Depending on the elected position, you may have an official government web page. Use the traffic that would have gone to your old website and send it there for the benefit of constituents.

Shutting down your site for good

A most common – and unfortunate – end to many campaign websites is that they are left untouched until the domain name or hosting period ends.

There are a few downsides to completely shutting down your online presence:

- Someone else can pick up the domain name, and you may have a tough time getting it back.

- You will have no control over a new website that someone creates with your lapsed domain name.

- All the links that you built up over the last campaign will now go nowhere since the website is gone. There is no guarantee that those links will still exist when you revive your website (assuming you have not let your domain name lapse before then).

Even if you want to completely shut everything down, consider keeping the domain name active - especially if the domain name matches the candidate's name. Keeping a domain name registered is a nominal cost, and it keeps the name in your possession.

If you decide to let go of your website, be sure to copy and back up your site content. You may want to unsubscribe from any email lists and send out a final message to your contact list that the site will be going dark. When you are sure everything has been taken care of, give notice to your hosting company that you are finished with the website.

There's nothing more sad than on old,
abandoned campaign website.

Shut down your email accounts

Let anyone in your campaign who has an email account know that the accounts will be shut down soon. Users should unsubscribe from any newsletters, alert their contacts, and perhaps make backups of any important emails.

Set up forwarders for your permanent email accounts, so you get copies of all emails going forward. That way, if you need to shut down services or recover passwords tied to specific email addresses, you can get copies of those messages.

Delete or suspend social media accounts

Delete your social media accounts if you are finished with them. Do this *before* you shut down your website and campaign email. If you forget your passwords and you've deleted your email addresses, you'll be out of luck. You may need updated login information from campaign members who have been running the accounts.

If you plan on keeping your campaign's social media accounts, change the passwords one last time and keep them safe.

Turn off ancillary services

Cancel or unsubscribe from any free or paid services. This may include email services, social media tools, fundraising platforms and so on.

Election Day and Beyond

If you have won (and we hope you do), congratulations! Depending on the elected position, your newly won office may already have an official web page waiting for you. Even so, consider keeping your old campaign website and social media accounts as a communications tool until the next election.

Even if you've lost, you can keep your online presence active. If you know you are going to run again, it makes sense to keep your campaign infrastructure intact.

Win or lose, take the time to make final updates after the election.

It takes hard work to win. There are no shortcuts.

A political campaign has always required planning and organizing, raising money, creating an issue platform, advertising, engaging voters, and a hundred other things. These days, a campaign also includes creating and managing an online presence. We hope the strategies and ideas in this book give you a head start and a plan of action that helps secure your Election Day victory.

Best of luck!

About Online Candidate®

Online Candidate provides affordable campaign website packages. Domain registration, hosting, a built-in content management system and tools are included. Accept online donations, recruit supporters, add events, upload photos, and more.

Visit us at OnlineCandidate.com.

Follow us online:

facebook.com/onlinecandidate

twitter.com/onlinecandidate

linkedin.com/company/online-candidate

Appendix A - Resources

Below is a list of resources to help you get started with your online campaign. The political service industry is an active one, with new services coming and going all the time. Please note that the author does not endorse these sites and is not responsible for their content.

Search Engine Accounts

Creating website accounts with the major search engines acts the same as a site submission. Website accounts allow you greater insight into how each engine indexes your website and provides additional tools.

Google Account (https://accounts.google.com) – Create a Google account to get started and access the other account functions below. All services are free.

- Google Alerts – Keep track of online mentions for names, phrases, and websites.

- Google Analytics – Track the who, what, and where of your website visitors.

- Gmail – Free email account.

- G Suite – Business version of Gmail, Google Calendar, Docs, and more.

- Google Search Console – Improve your site's visibility in Google search results; discover links, query traffic, and gain other information about your site.

- Google Ads – Google's pay per click advertising network.

- YouTube – Google's video service.

Bing Webmaster Tools
https://www.bing.com/toolbox/webmaster

Social Media Resources

Facebook.com - The largest social networking site in the world.

- https://www.facebook.com/pages/create/ - Create a new Page.
- https://www.facebook.com/help/ - Help center.
- https://newsroom.fb.com/ – News about the Facebook community.

Twitter.com – A popular micro-blogging site.

LinkedIn.com – Build and engage with your professional network.

YouTube.com – The largest video website on the web. Most political candidates who use video have a presence on this site.

Instagram.com - Photo-sharing app, owned by Facebook.

Pinterest.com – A popular site for displaying and sharing images with others.

Social Media Management Tools

Buffer.com - Social media scheduling, publishing, and analysis tool.

Hootsuite.com – Monitor conversations, compile reports, and post to multiple social media networks at one time.

TweetDeck.com - Real-time Twitter tracking, organizing, and engagement.

Warble.co - Daily email alerts for Twitter. Track keywords, phrases, #hashtags @mentions and more.

Social Media Tracking Tools

Mention.com

SproutSocial.com

URL Shorteners

These tools shorten links so they will fit better in Twitter posts, within emails, or for other purposes. Some services and tools have their own built-in shorteners.

bitly.com

tiny.cc

File Storage Tools

Dropbox - https://www.dropbox.com/

Google Docs - https://docs.google.com

Microsoft Office Web Apps - https://products.office.com/en-us/free-office-online-for-the-web

Online Communication Platforms

Slack.com

Basecamp.com

Trello.com

Video Conferencing Services

- GoToMeeting.com

- Google Hangouts (limited participants)
- Skype.com (limited participants)
- Webex.com
- Zoom.us

Video Hosting Sites

Sproutvideo.com

Vimeo.com

Youtube.com

Wistia.com

Political Fundraising Services

There are a growing number of political fundraising services. These were selected for cost, ease of use, and for meeting the needs of local campaigns. Vendor specifics are subject to change.

ActBlue.com – Popular Democratic fundraising service.

Anedot - Donation and payment system for non-profits, political campaigns, and causes. Integrates with multiple services.

FundHero.io – Fundraising service with built-in Contact Relationship Management system.

NGPVan.com - Democratic fundraising service.

PayPal Donations - Many smaller campaigns still use PayPal, but it lacks many tools and features of political-specific services.

RaiseTheMoney.com - Provides campaigns and organizations with a streamlined way to accept online contributions.

WinRed.com – Fundraising platform for conservative and center-right groups.

Online Marketplace Services

Cafepress.com

Zazzle.com

Spreadshop.com

Email Messaging Vendors

The best way to get a solid, responsive email list is to grow it yourself.

AWeber.com – Free to use. Includes features like autoresponders and split testing.

MailChimp.com - Free for up to 2,000 addresses. Limited features and send ability with free plan.

MailerLite.com - Free for up to 1,000 addresses. Includes a library of app integrations.

SendGrid.com – Can accommodate larger lists and higher volume.

Voter Data Services

L2political.com - Voter analysis, voter mapping and selection tools.

TargetSmart.com – Offers several voter and list services.

TheDataGroup.com – Offers voter lists, email, and phone data.

TowerData.com – Get information from your existing email list subscribers to segment your messages.

Campaign Software and Apps

Campaign software services include voter information, segmentation, field operation apps, and more.

BallotReady.org - Provides personalized, nonpartisan information to voters in all 50 states. Includes online voting tools for voter and candidates.

Ecanvasser.com - Manage door-to-door canvassing remotely.

EventBrite.com - Create, manage, and promote events.

Handraiser.com - Identifies, activates, and measures the participation of every voter.

OutreachCircle.com - Friend-to-friend outreach platform that enables supporters to identify and connect with eligible voters.

Votesharp.biz - A constituent communications tool specifically for state and local elected officials and candidates.

SummitPoliticalApps.com - Mobile apps for political campaigns.

Contact Relationship Managers

EveryAction.com

Fundhero.io

Hubspot.com

pipedrive.com

SalsaLabs.com

Voice and Text Messaging Services

Callfire.com

CallHub.io

Rumbleup.com

Textmarks.com

Trumpia.com

Online Advertising Services

Besides these services, there are other independent firms that specialize in digital advertising.

Social media advertising

facebook.com/advertising/

business.instagram.com/advertising/

youtube.com/yt/advertise/

Pay-per-click services

ads.google.com

Retargeting services

PerfectAudience.com

Retargeter.com

facebook.com/business/goals/retargeting

IP targeting services

Eltoro.com

OnlineCandidate.com

Free press release websites

OnlinePRNews.com – Allows for embedded link.

PRLog.org

Website Tools

Search engine accounts

google.com/accounts

bing.com/toolbox/webmaster

Analytics

analytics.google.com

ga-dev-tools.web.app/campaign-url-builder/

Website policy generators

Privacy Policy Generator

bennadel.com/coldfusion/privacy-policy-generator.htm

FreePrivacyPolicy.com

freeprivacypolicy.com/free-privacy-policy-generator.php

PrivacyPolicyOnline.com Terms of Service Generator

privacypolicyonline.com/terms-of-service-generator/

Video editors

Camtasia Studio (echsmith.com/video-editor.html) - Screen recorder and video editor. Allows you to record anything that you can view on your computer screen including software applications, web pages, PowerPoint presentations and more.

OpenShot.org - Free and open-source video editor for Linux, Mac, and Windows.

SRecorder.com - Free software that records your PC desktop at a high video and audio quality.

Online surveys

SurveyMonkey.com

SurveyGizmo.com

Graphics Resources

Free or low-cost graphics tools and resources.

Canva.com – *Recommended*. A graphic-design tool website that provides access to over a million photographs, graphics, and fonts.

FreeImages.com - All free for personal and commercial use

Gimp.org – A freely distributed piece of software for such tasks as photo retouching, image composition and authoring.

loc.gov/free-to-use/ - Library of Congress digital collections that are free to use.

Pexels.com - Free, high-quality images.

Pixabay.com - Free, high-quality images.

Photopea.com – Web-based graphics editor that is similar to Photoshop. Free and paid version.

Photoshop.com – Free trial version available of the popular graphics software.

PicResize.com – Free image resizer tool.

Unsplash.com - Free, high-quality images.

commons.wikimedia.org/wiki/Main_Page – Wikipedia Commons is a collection of freely usable media files.

Campaign Town Hall Services

A campaign town hall is a coordinated event in which one or more speakers may interact with their audience online.

MaestroConference.com

TeleTownHall.com

TelephoneTownHallMeeting.com

Campaigning Resources

CandidateBootCamp.com/blog

CampaignsAndElections.com

DigitalPoliticsRadio.com

ElectionTools.org

Epolitics.com

TheCampaignWorkshop.com/blog

Candidate Training Programs

Below is a list online training programs to help political candidates run a successful campaign.

American Majority - americanmajorityonline.org

Arena - arena.run

Asian Pacific American Institute for Congressional Studies (APAICS) - apaics.org

Blue Institute - theblue.institute

Collective PAC - collectivepac.org

Dare to Run - daretorun.org/upcoming-webinars

Democracy for America (DFA) - democracyforamerica.com/site/events/category/online-trainings

Elevate - ncil.org/elevate

Emerge America - emergeamerica.org/candidate-training

Emily's List - emilyslist.org/run-to-win/trainings

Federal Election Commission Training - fec.gov/help-candidates-and-committees/trainings

Higher Heights for America - higherheightsforamerica.org/webinars

IGNITE - ignitenational.org/calendar

National Democratic Training Committee - traindemocrats.org

National Women's Political Caucus - nwpc.teachable.com/p/nwpc-online-campaign-training

Ready to Run cawp.rutgers.edu/education_training/ready_to_run/overview

Re:Power - repower.org/events

Running Start - runningstartonline.org

She Should Run - sheshouldrun.org/explore/road-to-run

Women's Public Leadership Network - training.womenspublicleadership.net

The Campaign School at Yale - tcsyale.org

Podcasts

Listen as campaign professionals and successful candidates reveal winning strategies. You can listen to these podcasts through their websites or subscribe to them through your favorite podcast app.

Digital Politics with Karen Jagoda

Digitalpoliticsradio.com

Since 2007, this show has highlighted the impact of new technologies on the campaign landscape, online fundraising, digital means of persuasion and getting out the vote.

Elected. The Podcast.

Electedpodcast.com/season1

This podcast shows what running for office, as a woman, is really like.

How To Run for Office

Mycampaigncoach.com/how-to-run-for-office-podcast/

This series focuses on winning election campaigns. Though the series ended in 2019, there is plenty of useful material for local candidates.

Running for Office Podcast Series

Americanmajority.org/resources/running-for-office-podcasts/

This series is from 2010 but provides a good roadmap for candidates over its 22 episodes.

Running for Office as an Online Candidate

Onlinecandidate.com/articles/running-for-office-podcast

Covers topics for candidates who want to leverage the web to help win their election.

Voter Registration Tools and Websites

Electiontools.org - Free resources for election officials.

Rockthevote.org - Registration platform tool and resources.

Vote.org - Technology to simplify political engagement and increase voter turnout. Includes free and paid tools.

Voteamerica.com – Voter registration information and tools.

Wecanvote.us - Voter registration information and tools.

Appendix B - Checklists

Here are checklists and worksheets you can use to help pull the pieces together for a solid online campaign plan.

Account Checklist

Account / Username / Password

Personal Accounts

___ Facebook _____ / _____

___ Twitter _____ / _____

___ _____ _____ / _____

___ _____ _____ / _____

___ _____ _____ / _____

Campaign Accounts

___ Google _____ / _____

___ Facebook _____ / _____

___ Twitter _____ / _____

___ YouTube _____ / _____

___ Campaign website _____ / _____

___ Personal website _____ / _____

___ Bing _____ / _____

Other

_____

_____

_____

Administrator Checklist

Create a list or spreadsheet of people with access to your online accounts. This should be kept updated throughout the campaign.

Name: _____
Contact Info: _____
Roles: _____
Access Notes: _____
Platform / Username / Password(s):

_____
_____
_____
_____

Name: _____
Contact Info: _____
Roles: _____
Access Notes: _____
Platform / Username / Password(s):

_____
_____
_____
_____

Name: _____
Contact Info: _____
Roles: _____
Access Notes: _____
Platform / Username / Password(s):

_____
_____
_____
_____

Online Campaign Checklist

This list should be modified as needed and incorporated into your campaign calendar. Some items may need to be done multiple times throughout a campaign.

Pre-campaign:

___ Reserve your website domain name.

___ Create a campaign Google account.

___ Begin monitoring online mentions about the candidate, opponent, and important issue keywords.

___ Create personal Facebook profile, begin building friend network.

___ Create LinkedIn profile, begin building connections.

___ Create social bookmark accounts. Backlink profiles/related material to them.

___ Identify and follow local political blogs and local online outlets including local political sites and frequent commenters.

___ Begin putting together initial website content.

___ Begin building contact/email list from volunteer information at in-person events.

___ Create campaign Facebook page.

___ Create campaign Twitter account.

___ Create campaign YouTube, and other social media accounts you will use.

Site launch:

___ Before launch, run through campaign website pre-launch checklist.

___ Syndicate site launch press release.

___ Add initial video(s) to YouTube account.

___ Announce campaign to social media followers/friends.

___ Use website link in all future print materials and broadcast advertising.

___ Notify email list.

___ Backlink site and content to social media accounts.

___ Begin online advertising, if planned.

Throughout campaign:

___ Regularly update website content.

___ Monitor and engage online content about the race.

___ Recruit new supporters/enlist members online and through in-person events.

___ Write and syndicate online press release prior to and after each event.

___ Add new supporters to email list after each event.

___ Add campaign commercials to YouTube account.

___ Add interviews to YouTube account.

___ Add event videos to YouTube account.

___ Add podcasts to YouTube account.

___ Ask supporters to 'friend' you through social networks.

___ Solicit volunteers via email and social networks.

___ Solicit donations via email and social networks.

___ Solicit donations via email/social network following each major event.

___ Reach out to local bloggers and important online outlets.

___ Continue online advertising. Test and target.

Run-up to Election Day:

___ Expand online advertising presence to local online audience.

___ Encourage supporters to promote the campaign through their own social network contacts.

___ Final push for volunteers.

___ Final fundraising appeals.

___ Send final voting reminders through email, social networking, website, text, and other available channels.

___ Suspend email autoresponders to prevent out-of-date messaging post-election.

Post-Election Day:

___ Update website with post-election message.

___ Post-election update to mail list and social networks.

___ Shut down social media accounts and services.

___ Suspend or reconfigure email list services.

___ Shut down campaign email accounts/reset forwarders.

___ Shut down or reconfigure campaign website for future use.

Social Media Post Checklist

Make sure each of your social media updates are created properly. Use social media tools to help streamline your updates.

___ Is the post informational or engaging?

___ Is it written well? Not too long, not too brief. Spell check?

___ Are links in the post correct? Landing pages correct?

___ Could the post be more visual with images, video, or slides?

___ Could the message be targeted to a specific audience?

___ Is the post content optimized for each social media platform you are posting to?

___ Should hashtags be included for additional exposure?

___ If this is a repost, is it too soon or too often?

___ Is this post fine for anyone to see? Is there anything that might come back to bite you?

___ Are you prepared to reply to comments or messages about the post?

___ Has the post been added to your social media records for tracking?

Campaign Website Design Worksheet

Site name (on site header):

_____

Slogan (on site header):

_____

Preferred colors (send sample campaign materials if they exist):

_____

Other notes for header design:

_____

_____

Domain name choice (in order of preference):

1) _____

2) _____

3) _____

What other websites do you like/dislike when creating the look of your campaign website? What elements stand out?

Additional notes (features, functionality required):

Campaign Website Content Worksheet

Home Page:

      Content file name: _____

      Image file names and captions:

Biography/Resume:

      Content file name: _____

      Image file names and captions:

Issues/Positions:

      Content file name: _____

      Image file names and captions:

Campaign News:

      Content file name: _____

      Image file names and captions:

Endorsements:

      Content file name: _____

      Image file names and captions:

Voter Registration Information:

    Content file name: _____

    Image file names and captions:

Contact/Support Page:

    Content file name: _____

    Image file names and captions:

Volunteer:

    Content file name: _____

    Image file names and captions:

Donate:

    Content file name: _____

    Image file names and captions:

Other:

    Privacy/Terms of Use file: _____

Website Launch Checklist

Before going live, you should make sure your site looks and functions properly. This is a non-technical checklist of important items.

___ Design looks good and colors are complementary.

___ Design is consistent throughout site.

___ Pages are simple in layout and design.

___ Regular fonts are used for the text.

___ Content is clear and consistent.

___ Contact information is correct.

___ Proper disclaimers are added.

___ Important content is above the fold or near top of page.

___ Long content has been broken up.

___ Images reinforce the content.

___ Every page has been proofread for grammar and spelling.

___ Visitors can find what they are looking for with no more than two clicks from the home page.

___ The navigation is simple to use.

___ 'Alt' descriptions on images.

___ All links lead to the correct destination.

___ All email addresses on the site are correct.

___ All forms are active and have been tested.

___ Donation links work properly.

___ Email sign-up forms work properly.

___ The site loads quickly under any web connection.

___ Old pages created during site construction have been removed.

Campaign Email Checklist

Email list setup

___ Begin contact/email list from volunteered information at in-person events.

___ Segment contacts to enhance reporting data.

___ Select your email system or vendor.

___ Create online signup forms for website.

___ Set up initial confirmation message.

___ Create follow-up autoresponder messages.

___ During the campaign, test send times and subject lines to improve open rates.

___ Segment messages to specific users based on interest or participation.

___ Track open and click rates for response.

___ Shut down autoresponders before the campaign ends so subscribers do not get messages post-election.

___ Maintain contact post-election with supporters.

Email message checklist

___ Has the message been proofread by several people?

___ Do all the links work?

___ Has the email been tested to be sure it appears right in multiple email readers?

___ Will the recipient's name appear in the salutation?

___ Is there a narrative behind the message?

___ Does the message appeal to emotion?

___ Does the narrative create urgency? Why does the reader need to act NOW?

___ Is this message different than others you've sent?

___ Are there file attachments with this message? If so, remove them, upload them to your website and include a link in the body of the message.

___ Is there an 'ask' (for a donation, to view a video, forward to a friend, etc.)?

___ Does the email landing page work? Is it effective?

___ Are any required disclaimers missing from the email or landing page?

___ Is your campaign information on the bottom of the email?

___ Is there a way for the recipient to unsubscribe?

Online Fundraising Checklist

___ Establish a campaign bank account.

___ Are you aware of donor rules and limitations for your state or location?

___ Payment processor selected.

___ Is there a plan in place to allow for recurring donations? Is it set up to finish at the end of the campaign?

___ Donation forms properly embedded/linked to site?

___ Donation linked/integrated to social media accounts and email templates?

___ Donor rules or limitations clearly posted on or with donation forms?

___ Separate forms set up or ready to go for specific drives?

___ Tracking in place to determine what drives donations? Analytics set up?

___ Email, print, and other campaigns to drive donors in place?

___ Donor tracking and recording procedures in place?

___ Follow-up and thank-you procedures in place?

Specific Support Requests

These are requests for action that your campaign can make of supporters:

___ Forward email newsletters to other interested parties.

___ Recruit followers via email or through social networks.

___ Visit and comment on content, such as news stories, videos, or viral campaigns.

___ Put up yard signs.

___ Request a small donation in response to an outside event.

___ Request a donation for a specific promotion.

___ Attend campaign events.

___ Volunteer at local offices.

___ Work a phone bank.

___ Connect with neighbors via door-to-door canvassing or hosting events.

___ Create or submit their own content such as blog posts or online videos.

___ Notify others about absentee ballots and rules.

___ Provide rides to voters who cannot get to the polls.

___ Requests for volunteers to drive voters to the polls.

___ Get Out The Vote!

___ Get Out The Vote! (Not a typo - it is just *that* important.)